WRITING
ONLINE

Second Edition

D1789975

WRITING ONLINE

Second Edition

A Student's Guide to the Internet and World Wide Web

Eric Crump
University of Missouri, Columbia

Nick Carbone
Colorado State University

Houghton Mifflin Company   Boston   New York

Sponsoring Editor Jayne Fargnoli
Assistant Editor Jennifer Roderick
Project Editor Elena Di Cesare
Associate Production/Design Coordinators
    Deborah Frydman, Jodi O'Rourke
Manufacturing Manager Florence Cadran
Marketing Manager Nancy Lyman

Printed in the U.S.A.

Library of Congress Catalog Card Number: 97-75564

ISBN: 0-395-89227-9

456789-SB-04 03 02

CONTENTS

PART FOUR   RESOURCES

16 Learning Online: A List of Resources   134

PREFACE

With the Internet in a period of exponential growth, information about the Internet is burgeoning as well. Yet this information can be difficult to manage and use. Our goal in writing this book is to help writing students and teachers ride the Internet wave to their advantage. A certain amount of frustration is to be expected when encountering an unfamiliar environment, especially a rapidly changing one like the Net. (We've experienced our share.) We hope this guide will help you learn the ways of the Internet more quickly than you would on your own.

This guide is not intended to answer every single question you might have about Internet tools and culture. There are too many local variables that we have no way of anticipating. The Net itself changes so fast that it is impossible to create a perfectly stable source of information and instruction. The best operating instructions for the Net are actually on the Net and are revised continually. We have provided information about how to find many help files and guides, but the best way to learn the technical, social, and educational ways of the Net is to dive right into it.

From that perspective, this book is a starting point on your journey. We will do our best to help you make the transition. After you have read the book, we encourage you to visit our web site, where you can post new information, questions, clarifications, and stories about life as students and teachers. More importantly, the web site allows you to interact with us and, in the process, to help improve the book.

The *Writing Online* web site is at the Houghton Mifflin College Division home page: http://www.hmco.com/college.

For anyone who does not have access to the Web, the authors and editors can be reached via e-mail at college_english@ hmco.com.

Changes to the Second Edition

Our main goal in revising *Writing Online* was to provide relevant and timely information by keeping up with the changing state of the Internet. We also wanted to streamline the book to make sure it remains both accessible and economical. To do this, we deleted material that is generally considered outdated such as Lynx, gopher, Mosaic, MacWeb, and WinWeb. Although this information may still be useful, it is not as vital as it once was. We then added material on aspects of the online world that are becoming increasingly important. The key additions to the second edition include:

- A new chapter on writing collaborative hypertext
- Brand new activities—three per chapter—on the book's web site
- Completely updated advice on citing Internet sources, reflecting the latest information on MLA, APA, and Chicago styles
- Guidance on using Fetch, a popular FTP program for Macintosh computers
- Expanded information on searching the Web, including the latest search engines

Organization of *Writing Online*

This guide is organized by concepts and specific tools. It is helpful to think of the Internet both as a technical construct—a technological medium made up of communication and information tools—and as a social construct—an environment of newly emerging social and educational conventions. We begin our discussion of the Internet by focusing on its social and educational context.

We have used certain conventions in this book to make it easier to use. For example, when we instruct you to type something, it will appear like this:

Type **this**

Internet examples appear in a special typeface to represent what you will see on-screen, like this:

This is an example of on-screen text.

Introduction

This section provides a foundation for using the tools described in subsequent sections. It offers guidance on the evolving culture of the Net, its relevance to writing students, and the acceptable norms of behavior known as "netiquette."

How To's

This section contains chapters that take you through the basic steps for using the most common tools on the Net, including:

- **Electronic Mail**   is perhaps the most common method of communicating on the Internet
- **Mailing Lists**   allow groups of people to discuss matters of common interest
- **Telnet**   allows people to use resources at other sites on the Net almost as if they were at each site
- **File Transfer Protocol (FTP)**   sends and receives files from one computer to another
- **World Wide Web Browsers**   use a hypertextual system of finding, receiving, and publishing information on the Net
- **Multiple-User Environments (MOOs)**   provide real-time communication and offer possibilities for creating and extending the virtual environment

We've tried at every possible opportunity to make our explanations and examples relevant to the interests of writing students. The examples lead you to resources that we hope will prove both interesting and useful in your studies. And they not only teach you how to use a particular tool, but also introduce you to the online writing community.

Research

This section covers the subjects of plagiarism, copyright, and source citation. These things are difficult enough to understand in the stable world of print—imagine how complex they become in the changeable world of the Net! New capabilities introduced by new technologies confuse the issues surrounding research. This section of the book attempts to shed some light on the complexity of online research and to help you adapt new tools to an old function. We offer practical advice and guidance on how to avoid plagiarism, respect copyright, and properly cite sources.

Resources

The Resources section expands on what is covered in the How To's section. It provides instruction on how to use the new tools you have learned and cites online sources for additional information.

Glossary

The Internet has its own special vocabulary that can be difficult to understand. The Glossary section of this book is a good introduction to many of the terms specific to the computing and network worlds. This is another section that may lend itself to collaborative extension via the book's web site.

Acknowledgments

We would like to express our deep appreciation to the many people who contributed to the development of this book. First, of course, a nod and a hug to our families—Amy, Flannery, and Quincy Crump, and Barbara Crowley-Carbone and Nicole and Emma Carbone—who graciously tolerated our obsession with the Net and our preoccupation with the book. We owe immeasurable debt to our colleagues on the Net, a bright and supportive group of teachers, students, and scholars. Everything we know about the Net is a direct result of working in such a rich learning environment with such terrific people. We are grateful to the wonderful and very patient people at Houghton Mifflin, especially George Kane and Jennifer Roderick, who helped us initiate this project and who strongly influenced its shape. Elena Di Cesare, Rebecca Bennett, and Deborah Frydman worked on the production of the book, and Stewart Jester helped set up the web site. Many people provided us with useful reviews: Kris Bair, Fort Hays State University (KS); Geoffrey Chase, Northern Arizona State University; Yuet-Sim D. Chiang, University of California, Berkeley; Alexander Friedlander, Drexel University (PA); Karen R. Hamer, Pittsburg State University (KS); Roger Johnson, Lewis-Clark State College (ID); Deborah Balzhiser Morton, University of Minnesota; John Peterson, University of California, Irvine; Peter R. Vanderhoof, Peninsula College (WA); and Janice R. Walker, University of South Florida. Special thanks to A. Dean Fontenot, Texas Tech University, who ensured the book's technical accuracy. And finally, we would like to thank you. We hope that readers of this book will use it to find their way online, resulting in productive new connections and collaborations.

Eric Crump
Nick Carbone

1

Introduction to the Online World

1.1 A World Within a World

It is bigger than any nation. It is as small as a cozy booth in a neighborhood café. By some accounts, its population is growing faster than the world's. By other accounts, its population estimates are grossly inflated. Depending on your perspective, it can either bring about social revolution or support the status quo. It contains vast quantities of information though finding the right information at the right time is not always a simple matter. It fosters intelligent discussion of issues, mindless prattle, and the sinister dealings of society's lunatic fringe. It liberates and enslaves. It is home to paradox and disorientation, to joy and excitement, to hyperbolic rhetoric and misinformation. It is the online world, the social environment that resides in the global network of people using computers to communicate. Right now the most dynamic part of the online world is the Internet.

Trying to capture the Internet in words reminds us of the parable of the blind men trying to describe an elephant. The one who grabbed the tail was sure the beast resembled a rope. The one who wrapped his arms around a thick leg was sure that it was very similar to a tree. The one who latched onto the trunk concluded that the animal was related to the snake. Likewise, the Internet, or Net for short, is a different critter depending on which piece of it you happen to grab.

1

1.2   The Internet

The Internet is a vast system of interconnected computer networks. These networks — distinct online worlds in themselves — connected to the Internet vary widely in size (geographic area and population), bandwidth (information volume), technological sophistication, and purpose. What holds them together is not a central authority but a central principle: cooperation — both technical and social. Administrators of each network agree to use certain technical protocols that allow diverse and otherwise incompatible machinery to interact, opening electronic conduits for almost any kind of information imaginable. The result is a networked system that no one owns but to which everyone contributes.

Like its machinery, the culture of the Net is based on collaboration, cooperation, and sharing. If that sounds unrealistically idyllic, it is and it isn't. Along with nice collegial sharing and friendship, people are quick to share their anger, their cynicism, and their paranoia.

1.3   Internet History

Any extensive history of the Internet might start as far back as the introduction of the telegraph, the first use of electricity to communicate over distance. For our purposes, though, the history of the Internet begins in the early 1960s, in the heart of the cold war. The U.S. government became interested in developing a communication system that would survive a nuclear attack. The Defense Department's Advanced Research Projects Agency (ARPA) was called upon to create the system. Researchers realized that the system would have to be decentralized so that no one part was essential to the operation of the whole. The beginnings of the Internet began to take shape in the early 1970s when researchers and technologists at a handful of universities developed the protocol (which became TCP/IP, Transmission Control Protocol/Internet Protocol) that would allow different computer systems to communicate with one another. Until the late 1980s, the system was primarily used by university and government scientists and technologists.

However, as tools for communicating and sharing information became easier to use, the popularity of the Internet grew throughout society: in universities, businesses, libraries, and other organizations. And like the personal computer movement of the late 1970s, the use of the Internet has spread to the home. Businesses are the fastest growing users of the Net, and individuals are quickly following, ready (more or less) to begin shopping there for information, goods, and entertainment. Just as the telegraph led to the telephone, which quickly reshaped our entire society, the Internet appears poised to do the same, with perhaps even more profound implications.

1.4   Relevance to Writing Students

Writers are concerned with language and literacy, with the conventions and possibilities of creating art and communicating ideas with words. Literacy and technology are inextricably intertwined. Print technology has dominated language arts for the past few centuries, and our conceptions of literacy have been shaped by the features of that technology. The emergence of computer networks as venues for communication and community will affect the fundamental shapes of literacy. Writers and readers now must understand how communication and literary arts work in electronic environments that both resemble and differ from print.

Writing and reading tend to happen faster in network environments. As a result, writing tends to be more conversational and informal. People also generally write for smaller groups as opposed to the large audience of a print publication.

Print calls for precision and efficiency because writers are limited by the number of words or pages available in publications. Therefore, print generally involves refinement, revising the text in an effort to express the ideas in a concise and logical way. In online venues, writing comes to mean something different. It is more conversational because readers can respond immediately. Ideas develop as part of those interactions with others. Clarity evolves through continued interaction — accumulation rather than purification. And space for all those words, though not infinite, is cheap and vast.

At the same time, the sensibilities of print culture exert a strong influence on people as they move to electronic or Internet writing environments. In many cases, teachers and students find ways to make these new electronic writing tools perform the same functions old writing tools did.

The Internet is especially relevant to writers. We will provide instruction on how to use the most common Internet tools for finding information and bringing new information online, as well as for communicating with others. We will suggest ways to put those tools to good use and will point to locations and projects on the Internet that are designed for writers, such as online journals, electronic versions of books, student-run multimedia publications, sites for publishing student work, and courses taught online. We will also offer comments on the history and culture of the Net as we know it — the social environment in which these tools were developed and continue to evolve.

1.5   Expectations for This Book

Writing an introductory guide to the Internet is in some ways a task destined to fail — at least it will fail to satisfy readers who expect definitive descriptions that will apply year after year. We are working with a moving target, a world that is in the volatile and transformative early stage of life (and that's what we like about it). Be suspicious of anyone who claims to know the Truth of the online world, who presumes to reveal all its secrets. We claim only to describe as best we can the parts we know well — as they exist now while we write this book.

As for the tail and the trunk and all the parts between, well, discovery is part of the fun. The Internet is vast, and although people disagree on how vast, there is much to explore. We hope this book will be a good start for your exploration, and we invite you to share your experiences. In conjunction with Houghton Mifflin, we have set up a homepage on the World Wide Web for updates and for collecting reader feedback. You and other readers will learn things about the Internet and its resources for writers that we do not yet know. The address for the homepage is **http://www.hmco.com/**. This takes you to the Houghton Mifflin Company Homepage; from there, you will find a link to the page for *Writing Online*. You can also reach us by e-mail at **College_English@hmco.com**. And don't worry, if you skip to the chapters in this manual on the World Wide Web and e-mail, you will learn all you need to know about how to use these addresses.

2

Netiquette

2.1 Introduction

The word *netiquette* combines "net," short for "Internet," and "etiquette." Etiquette on the Internet, like etiquette everywhere else, works best when seasoned with a little tolerance, compassion, and humor. Good netiquette requires observing the customs of the Net, much as knowing the customs and habits of where you travel makes you more welcome. The Internet is foremost about bringing people together. As much as it is praised for the vast amounts of information available to users, that information is secondary to the people with whom you can communicate.

There are three general categories of netiquette: netiquette for using the Internet, netiquette for communicating on the Internet, and netiquette for acknowledging people and resources on the Internet. Like any set of rules or advice, following them requires good judgment. Much of the advice we outline here will also be covered in other sections of the book. For example, when we discuss e-mail in Chapter 4, you will read more about e-mail netiquette. Our purpose here is to give you in one section a compendium of the types of netiquette that help make the Internet a useful resource.

2.2   Netiquette for Using the Internet

Protect your privacy and that of others

First, remember that your e-mail is not secure. It can be read by system administrators or anyone who may have your password. To help protect your privacy, choose a password to your account that is a combination of numbers and characters that do not spell a word or common phrase. For example, TEA4TWO would be fairly easy to hack, whereas T&8GM44 would be much harder.

Learn and follow the acceptable use policy

Netiquette on use is usually described in acceptable use policies (AUPs) set forth by the company or service that provides your Internet access. For most of you reading this book, it will be policies set by your school. These may include limits on the amount of information you can store on your account, or limits on when you can use the Internet recreationally, as with MUDs (multiple user dungeons; also referred to as "dimensions" or "domains") or IRC (Internet Relay Chat), two tools associated with chatting and playing games.

Don't play when someone else needs to work

Although we can think of no academic computer network whose sole purpose is to be a virtual arcade, we haven't yet heard of one where there isn't some online game. Playing games is fine, as long as it's in moderation and does not interfere with the work of others.

Always get permission for exceptions to rules

Many teachers use software associated with games, like MUDs or MOOs (MUD — object oriented), as places for classes to meet online. Students also use these tools for research and to meet other scholars who are interested in the same academic subjects. The resource chapter in this manual lists educational MOOs you can visit. If your purpose in using tools normally associated with gaming is educational, that's wonderful. However, you should still follow your school's AUP unless you get permission to do otherwise. Many administrators will allow an exception if they understand how you are using the tools.

2.3   Netiquette for Communicating on the Internet

Stand by your words

You should always be accountable for what you write and say. Don't write or send anything on the Internet, or anywhere else for that matter, that you are not ready to stand by. This does not mean you cannot change your mind or eventually come around to another point of view. It means you should think about what you want to say, and say it as clearly as you can. On the Internet, you exist primarily in the words you write. What you say *is* who you are in an online world; it is the only way most people online will ever know you.

End e-mail with your name and address

People usually overlook this point of netiquette because they assume another user will be able to see or know their e-mail and name automatically. This is not always the case. Thus your name and address become important, especially when sending mail to a discussion list or to Usenet (an Internet-wide collection of discussion groups). Your address makes it easier for others to respond directly to you, but only if you include it at the end of your message.

Never leave the subject heading blank

Many people have software that automatically deletes messages without a subject heading. Others use their own personal filter — the delete key. Blank subject headings reduce your chances of being read; they cripple communication. The only time you will want a blank subject heading is when sending messages to some discussion list software, such as Listserv.

Cross-post appropriate messages only

Some messages you read might encourage you to forward them, for example, announcements of literary contests, internships, or job openings. Others might happen to coincide with a discussion you are having on another list or in another forum, say, a classroom. You should cross-post these latter types only if you are certain the writer would not mind; the best way to be certain is to get permission.

Practice frugality

We use the word *frugal* here, instead of the usual term *brevity*, to stress that we do not mean all messages must be short, but instead that all messages should try to use words as thoughtfully as possible for two reasons: people often have a lot of e-mail to sort through and may not bother to finish rambling messages, and being frugal increases your chances of being understood.

Strive for clarity

Clarity can suffer for any number of reasons. It is sometimes lost because the writer and reader do not share the same context or frame of reference. For example, on one list, a writer sent a message recommending an article in CCC. Many people on the list did not know CCC referred to a journal called *College Composition and Communication*. Some confusion is inevitable. However, there are steps you can take to keep it to a minimum.

Give yourself a minute to think about a message before you write it

Most electronic messages are written quickly; it is one of the charms of the medium. This is especially true for real-time (or simultaneous) discussions, such as MOOs and MUDs, where two or more users agree to log on to the Internet at the same time. People know that there will be more typos and misspellings because participants are literally writing as they think, and what they write is being read almost the instant it is keyed in.

However, in writing such as e-mail, Usenet, and World Wide Web discussion forums, messages are sent for others to read and respond to later. Since there is more of a time lag, people generally expect fewer errors than they do in real-time forums. When writing e-mail, try to take a moment to write the message first in your head.

Be tolerant of errors, including your own

Taking care to avoid errors is best. However, you do not want to write e-mail as if you were taking a test. You will write both good messages and embarrassing ones, so treat errors kindly. Never publicly correct someone for an error in spelling or punctuation, especially since many e-mail programs lack spell-checking software. If an error distorts the meaning of a message beyond your understanding, e-mail the writer privately and ask for clarification.

Use accurate summaries and judicious quoting

The Reply command on most e-mail and Usenet reader programs offers you a choice of including the original message in your reply. If you say yes, delete any portion of the original message that is not relevant. For example, if you are responding to only two sentences in a forty-sentence message, delete all but those two sentences. You can summarize the other thirty-eight sentences in a line or two if needed.

Keep cool if you've been flamed

A flame is a message that is full of invective, spit, and fury. Flames vary in heat and intensity, and some are actually unintentional. Flaming can change the atmosphere of an Internet community the way a mugging changes the atmosphere of a street. On some groups, flaming is to be expected. Anywhere politics or social policy is discussed, there are likely to be flames. The worst flames attack a person's character instead of his or her argument. Some Usenet groups are famous for their flame wars, pitched battles of e-mail invectives. According to Chuq Von Rospach's *A Primer on How to Work with the USENET Community,* one of the most common sources of flame wars is when people try to correct someone's grammar or punctuation.

Many times people feel they've been flamed when in fact no flame was intended. Take a moment to consider what was written, and respond to it thoughtfully and patiently. If you are unsure of what the author intended, ask. If you have been flamed, it is better to respond with wit and humor. Even if you get a particularly virulent flame, defend yourself with tact. Be sure to criticize the argument and not the person.

2.4   Netiquette for Acknowledging People and Resources on the Internet

The final area of netiquette has to do with attribution. Correct attribution of sources has always been important in academic writing. This is perhaps even more true for the Internet. Many sites offer online resources that can be downloaded and used as handouts. For example, Purdue University has an Online Writing Lab (OWL) that offers guides to grammar and punctuation. Students and teachers are welcome to download these, but are asked to keep the headings on so that others know the handouts originated at Purdue's OWL. Whenever you borrow from or refer to online sources, be sure to acknowledge them. If you are unsure of the attribution policy of a site, check with your instructor or e-mail the site administrator.

3

Preparing to Enter the Internet

3.1 A Word About Interface

In this chapter of *Writing Online*, we cover how to use different tools available to you on the Internet. The dilemma we face is having no way to anticipate all the varied types of access, computer software, and experience our readers will have. The term *interface* refers to the combination of all three of these. Your e-mail program might be easy to use — with many of the same kinds of point-and-click features you are familiar with in other computer applications — and you may feel comfortable navigating the screen it presents, using the commands, and sending mail. Or you might have a program that requires you to remember a number of commands that you will have to type. The different types of interface combinations, though not quite endless, are daunting.

3.2 Getting Help with Software

To begin using the Internet, you need to make sure you have the documentation that is available for the software you are using. If you are accessing the Net from an educational provider, you may have received some handouts and guides from campus computing support services. On most campuses, the department that sets up computers and manages user accounts will also provide help to users. You should write down the phone number and e-mail address of the user support services on your campus. Write the numbers in the front and back of this book; if you own your computer, tape the numbers near your screen. The first question to ask when you call is how to get any of the documentation they have for users.

3.3   Leave Time for Learning and Error

Preview your handouts

Once you have the handouts and other materials from your campus help center, you should read the directions *several times* before you begin an actual procedure. Bear in mind that reading the directions can be alienating at first since they often contain lots of computer jargon. Further, sometimes the directions make sense only as you are actually doing a procedure. Take your time and do the best you can; try not to be intimidated by excessive jargon or the need to use commands and procedures that seem as mysterious as a shaman's incantations. Follow the steps and see what happens.

Diagnose your mistakes

Mistakes fall into two general categories. The first is where you make the wrong choice, but the software thinks it is a valid choice. For example, you accidentally change an entry in your e-mail address book. As far as the computer is concerned, no error has been made. So for these kinds of mistakes, it's up to you to notice that something has gone wrong.

The second type of error occurs when you type in unacceptable data, and the software refuses to go on. For example, you enter the wrong password. Sometimes the software will repeat the step at which you made an error or flash an error message, in which case you would have a second chance to enter the data correctly. For example, if you make an error at the login prompt, the prompt will usually return, and you can try again. After a set number of tries without success, however, the program will usually disconnect you from that step, sending you back to the previous step.

Very often the latter type of error occurs with UNIX, a case-sensitive computer operating system common on the Internet. Case sensitive means you must type the command with *exact* capitalization. If the command to start your e-mail program is **pine**, but you type **Pine**, you will get an error message saying, "Command not found." Unfortunately, the error message will not say, "Sorry, but you need to retype the command with a lowercase p." You have to figure out your own mistake.

As you can see, computer software requires some precision from users. Software has only as much logic as a programmer gives it, and no programmer can anticipate every type of human error. You must learn the software's logic, or at least enough of it to make the software work.

> HELPFUL HINT: Always assume a system will be case sensitive, especially when using gopher (a menulike program used for moving among computers connected to the Internet), e-mail, Usenet, and the World Wide Web. If you type in an address in gopher or on the Web, type it exactly as it is given to you. In e-mail and Usenet, do the same.

When you are having trouble with software on the Internet, go slowly and write down what happens as well as any messages the software gives you. This way, when you ask for help, you'll be able to tell user support services exactly what happened.

3.4 Dealing with the Enormousness of the Internet

The Internet is so big, offers so many different ways of being accessed and traversed, that dealing with all the choices and excitement about the Internet is a task in itself. You do not need to know everything and try everything at once. There are learning curves to all that you will discover in this book. The slope of those curves and the time it takes you to ascend them depends on your computer experience and your ability to conceptualize what you are doing.

Create a mental picture

Much of the software you use will provide you with familiar metaphors — often in the form of icons — to help guide you. You probably already know some software metaphors: the screen is a desktop; your work is saved in a file and put in a folder; your e-mail has an in-box. To feel comfortable on the Internet, you need a mental picture that works for you, some image to help orient and ground yourself in a world that has no ground, only space — cyberspace.

4

Electronic Mail

4.1 Introduction

Electronic mail, or e-mail, remains the most popular way to use the Internet. We certainly recommend it as the best place to begin. With e-mail as a starting point, you can learn a lot about literature and writing, and, at the same time, learn about a very practical and necessary application. Yes, necessary. Familiarity with e-mail will be an expected skill in many of the employment markets, including the academic market. Knowing how to use e-mail will become as necessary as knowing how to use the telephone. If you stop to think of all the ways the telephone shapes your life — making appointments, checking in with friends, ordering take-out food, getting a date, conducting business — you'll get an idea of how important e-mail will become as a means of communication. We are so accustomed to telephones, we hardly think about them any more. In time, e-mail will become just as commonplace. But until that time, it helps to have an overview of e-mail as you prepare to use it.

4.2 The Speed of E-Mail

E-mail is not quite the same as postal mail, or what regular e-mail users call "snail mail" because of its slower delivery time. Half the fun of sending postal mail has always been the anticipation of a response. E-mail's speed accentuates anticipation and makes it exciting. There's nothing quite like sending a note to someone on the other side of the country (or the world for that matter) and having him or her write back that same day. What might take a week or so by snail mail could take no more than an hour by e-mail. It could conceivably occur faster — almost instantly — if the person happens to be reading his or her e-mail when you send the message. However, the rapid response time can create new kinds of pressures. Waiting a week to reply to snail mail is not at all unusual, but in e-mail it is a long time. So as you enter the world of e-mail and e-mail discussion lists, keep in mind the time factor and the expectation that response should come sooner rather than later.

Many students use e-mail because they have friends at other colleges who have it, and it's cheaper than a phone call. Others use it because they can contact professors or other students from their classes.

4.3 E-Mail Basics

To work comfortably with an e-mail program, you should know how to:

1. Make sense of e-mail lingo
2. Write an e-mail address
3. Use a subject line
4. Use the Reply command
5. End a message
6. Use an address book
7. Save messages into folders
8. Download and upload files to send by e-mail
9. Deal with spam messages

You can do more, but if you can manage these steps, in this approximate order, you will be well on your way to happy and productive e-mailing.

1. Making Sense of E-Mail Lingo

We've already mentioned the term *snail mail,* which refers to physical mail moved over land. Many e-mail terms refer to e-mail's speed. Others are born of a writer's need to make sure he or she is not being taken the wrong way. In the pursuit of the sometimes mutually exclusive goals of writing quickly and not being misunderstood, e-mail use has developed two phenomena: the acronym and the emoticon.

Acronym shorthand

Writers use acronyms as a shorthand in messages to save time and space. People also use acronyms for their catchiness. Acronyms indicate the writer is "in" on e-mail lingo. Here is a brief list. Often, if you ask someone what one of these means, you will be teased for being a "newbie," a new user on the Internet. Thus the desire to be "in."

BTW	by the way
FWIW	for what it's worth
FYI	for your information
IMO	in my opinion
IMHO	in my humble/honest opinion
TIA	thanks in advance
RTFM	read the f***ing manual
LOL	laughed or laughing out loud
ROTFL	rolling on the floor laughing
YMMV	your mileage may vary (This comes from the little disclaimer tacked onto auto advertisements. It usually means, "What I say may not apply for you.")

Smileys or emoticons

These are little drawings made with a sequence of typewriter keys. Writers place them at key points in their writing to help signal their intent. People especially rely on them when they want to be sure a point they are making will get across in the intended tone. Sometimes they are used for emphasis as well. Here are some of the most common ones.

:-)	A basic smiley. Some use it to indicate light sarcasm or humor. Occasionally, it is used to soften criticism. We've seen it used to express joy.
:)	A basic smiley without the nose — for people who like to conserve keystrokes.
;-)	A winking smiley. Often used to mean "just kidding."
:-(	A sad face. Sometimes used to show sympathy; sometimes used to reflect how the writer feels about a topic or issue.
:-0	An expression of surprise or shock.

:-|	An expression of grim determination or indifference depending on the context.
:->	An expression of sarcasm or archness.
>;->	A winking, arch devil. Chances are a lewd remark was made.

In the netiquette overview in Chapter 2, we talked about being careful with your words. Many guides will advise you to use smileys when attempting sarcasm or irony because doing so will help eliminate or reduce misunderstandings. This may or may not be the case. How and when you use smileys depends on how much fun you are having with your writing and who your audience is.

E-mail does have its complications. The high volume of e-mail forces quick reading and frequent deleting of messages. People often gripe about overflowing in-boxes containing many messages that are a waste of time, although the truth is they would not be overwhelmed if they weren't on so many lists. As you work in e-mail, keep in mind that from time to time you will be annoyed by these messages. The best thing to do is :-) and GOWI (get on with it — an acronym we just made up).

2. Writing an E-Mail Address

E-mail addresses are made up of two parts separated by an @ sign. The first part is the username; often it's the login name of the user. This always comes to the left of the @. To the right of the @ is the domain name. Take, for example, the e-mail address for Nick:

Domain names are used as part of the Internet's domain name system (DNS), a method of naming host computers that access the Internet. This helps make remembering Internet addresses easier. One thing to note when sending e-mail is the different endings domain names can take. Here are some domain name endings and the sites they indicate:

| edu | for *edu*cational site |
| gov | for *gov*ernment site |

mil	for *mil*itary site
com	for a business or person accessing from a *com*mercial site
ca	for *Ca*nada
net	often for an Inter*net* service provider
uk	for the *U*nited *K*ingdom

It sometimes helps compare an e-mail address to a postal address. Using Nick as an example, we notice that a postal address has a consistent hierarchy:

Postal Address	Elements
Nick Carbone	Name
c/o English Department	Academic Department
UMass, Amherst	Institution
Amherst, MA 01002	City, State, and Zip Code

The same hierarchy applies to an e-mail address:

E-Mail Address	Elements
nickc	Login Name
@	Separator
english	Academic Department
umass	Institution
edu	Educational Site

3. Using a Subject Line

Subject lines are very important in e-mail because they tell what the message is about. A good subject line helps the reader make sense of the purpose of the e-mail. Accurate subject lines are very important in distribution lists and bulletin boards that have many users. The subject line identifies which conversational "thread" the message is part of, allowing users who aren't participating in that strand to delete those messages. If you change the topic of discussion, you should also change the subject line.

4. Using the Reply Command

Every e-mail program we have ever heard of has a Reply command. It allows a user to press a letter (usually r) or some other key to automatically address an e-mail message to the sender, whether he or she is on an e-mail discussion list or a personal correspondent. Using the Reply command is so easy that many users do it automatically, without thinking about when they should use it. Knowing when to use the Reply command essentially means knowing how to read the headers — information that comes at the top of a message — on your e-mail. Headers will tell you where a message will go if you use the Reply command. Consider the following header as it appears in the Elm e-mail program:

Date: Mon, 14 Jul 1997 11:13:15 -0400 (EDT)
From: Nick Carbone <nickc@english.umass.edu>
Subject: Re: MOOmeeting
To: Eric Crump <wleric@showme.missouri.edu>

This header comes from a message from Nick to Eric on July 14. It's direct e-mail and replying will automatically send a message to Nick. The next header is from a message Eric sent to Rhetnet-L, a discussion list for rhetoric and writing.

Date: Fri, 28 Feb 1997 13:56:43 -0600 (CST)
Reply-To: RHETNET-L@lists.missouri.edu
Sender: owner-RHETNET-L@lists.missouri.edu
From: Eric Crump <wleric@SHOWME.MISSOURI.EDU>
To: RhetNet list <RHETNET-L@lists.missouri.edu>
Subject: Re: universities — RIP
X-Sender: wleric@sp2n09.missouri.edu

The key to using the Reply command is knowing where it will send your reply. Most of the mail sent directly to you will not have a Reply-to line (see the first example). For mail that comes to you via a list, you will usually see a Reply-to option. Sending a message to a list when you think it is going to only one person can be embarrassing. If you were on RHETNET-L and wanted to reply directly to Eric, perhaps with something only he and you should know, you would want to make sure the message was going only to him and not to RHETNET-L. The way to tell this is to first note in your header that the message comes from the list and not directly from Eric to you. Second, make sure that you address your reply to Eric by typing in his address at your e-mail program's To: prompt.

5. Ending a Message

Always end a message with your name and e-mail address. As simple a rule as this is, people often forget it.

Since interfaces and e-mail programs vary so widely, you cannot always assume your e-mail address will automatically be visible to the person reading your message. If the message is sent directly to the person, this is less of an issue because he or she can usually rely on the Reply command to automatically send a message back to you. But there are times when for some reason the Reply command does not work and the person may need to double-check your address. It's always more convenient if he or she sees your address, so always close your message with it.

Signature files

Many regular e-mail users create signature files. A signature file, sometimes called "sig" for short, is a file that contains at least your name and e-mail address. It is placed where your e-mail program can find it and is automatically appended to each message you write, thus assuring that you always end your messages with your name and e-mail address. Many signature files are more elaborate than just containing a name and e-mail address. They may also consist of home and work snail mail addresses, phone numbers (though we advise against this), a favorite quote, a disclaimer that the views expressed are the person's own and not his or her employer's, and ASCII art (pictures made from an arrangement of letters and characters). A good signature file works as effectively as a business card. However, signature files can become too elaborate and long. A good rule of thumb is to keep a signature file to five lines or fewer.

Here's what a signature file might look like:

```
*  Nick Carbone        Marlboro College              *
*  nickc@marlboro.edu  Marlboro, VT 05344            *
*                                                    *
*  If you can touch your toes without bending your knees,  *
*  you don't watch nearly enough TV.                 *
```

6. Using an Address Book

Each e-mail program will differ in how it creates, edits, and uses an address book, and whether it even calls the feature an address book. Elm, for example, calls this feature an "alias file." Eudora calls it "nicknames." An address book lets you create a shorthand for frequently used e-mail addresses so that you do not have to type in the full address every time you send a message. Nick exchanges mail with Eric once or twice a week; therefore, he's entered Eric's name and e-mail address in his alias file. When he writes to Eric, he uses the command for mailing, and when prompted for an e-mail address, he types **ec**. The e-mail program automatically adds wleric@showme.missouri.edu. Address books can also be used to include addresses for e-mail discussion lists. Furthermore, a group of addresses can be collected under one larger address to create a distribution list. Address books are the e-mail equivalent of speed dialing.

7. Saving Messages into Folders

Most e-mail programs allow you to sort messages into folders. For example, you might create a folder for each discussion list you are on. If you receive a message you wish to reply to later or save for some other reason, you can save it to a folder. When you use the folder system — and on most programs this is done by choosing the command to save the message — the program can be set, by going into an options or preferences menu, to suggest a folder name based on the name of the sender. Messages Nick receives from Eric are saved into a folder called wleric, the program's default name based on Eric's e-mail address. You can also choose a different name for a folder. For example, Nick has one folder called grammar where he saves messages that relate to the teaching of grammar.

8. Downloading and Uploading Files to Send by E-Mail

Downloading and uploading e-mail messages is most easily done by using ASCII, a standard for computer-generated characters, such as numbers, letters, and symbols. Most word processors will have a feature to save as text only. This option removes all formatting — bold, italics, underlining, set fonts — and saves your message as a plain text file. This allows the message to be sent and read in just about any word processor or e-mail program. There are other ways to send messages written in a program other than your e-mail program's text editor, but ASCII or text only is the easiest to learn.

Downloading and deleting messages are an important part of user netiquette. Cleaning your e-mail in-box makes sure your messages won't pile up and exceed the in-box's capacity. When your in-box is full, new messages will be rejected. Sometimes they will be sent back to the sender; sometimes they will get lost in cyberspace. In either case, you won't get the message. You will also tie up system resources. Each file takes up disc space, so many access providers limit each user to a fixed amount of space. This can be measured in total bytes, in total number of files, or in a combination of both. Regular housekeeping is one of the most important pieces of netiquette you can practice.

9. Dealing with Spam Messages

Spam in e-mail has nothing to do with the trademarked food product. Instead, it refers to a message that combines the worst aspects of telemarketing and door-to-door salespeople, or at least it feels that way when you receive it. Spam messages are indiscriminate intrusions into your e-mail, most often from a discussion list you may be on. Spammers like to target lists because the list does the work of spreading the message for them. Spam senders don't care that they are intruding into someone's e-mail; in fact, many secretly enjoy the mischief they cause. It's from this annoying and inane interruption that spam gets its name. The British comedy troupe Monty Python used to perform a recurring skit in which characters would burst out singing, "spam, spam, spam, spam, spam" over and over, bringing everything else going on in the skit to a stop.

Spams can often be identified from their subject lines: "Earn Big Money for Little Work," "1,500 Great Magazines." The easiest way to deal with spam is to simply delete the message and get on with your e-mail. Unfortunately, part of the spam phenomenon usually includes discussion of spam itself, which, in effect, increases the amount of spam. In other words, anyone can send spam to a discussion list, but only the list members can turn it into a prolonged nuisance by complaining on the list about it, turning spam into a kind of self-replicating spore.

Mailing Lists: Hosts for Discussion Groups and Online Communities

5.1 Introduction

Electronic mail may seem almost magical when compared to its print-based predecessor, postal mail. It is astoundingly faster and more convenient (once you learn how to make it work). But even electronic mail by itself pales in comparison to the power unleashed by electronic mailing lists, which greatly expand the ability to communicate with others over the Net using e-mail.

5.2 How Mailing Lists Work

Mailing lists are like regular bulk mail except they are faster and more flexible. Bulk mail is often used when someone (usually an advertiser or sweepstakes organizer) wants to reach many people with the same information. They may obtain lists of street addresses and use them to scatter huge quantities of their material in the wind. E-mail lists operate much the same way. When someone sends a note addressed to the list's e-mail address, the mailing software "explodes" the note, sending a copy to every subscriber.

How much listspace is on the Internet?

This simple question has a complicated answer. Thousands of mailing lists are on the Internet, perhaps 15,000 to 20,000, but that is only a guess. No one knows for sure how many there are because some are private (that is, not registered or indexed anywhere), and new ones are born every day. Few die. To give an example, in the fall of 1991, the University of Missouri-Columbia hosted about thirty-five public lists. As of the summer of 1997, it hosted 497, a 1,400 percent increase in less than 6 years. It's difficult to say whether this case is typical or not, but certainly the growth is impressive.

An increasing number of lists

Probably the main reason the number of lists continues to grow is that mailing list software is so flexible. Mailing lists can serve a wide range of purposes. Some support small private working groups; some host open discussions on any topic; some provide a place for intensely focused debate on specific issues; some serve as places to exchange data; and some are used mainly to disseminate information. Lists are used by corporations, politicians, scholars, researchers, and students. They serve as a means of communication for committees, classes, electronic publications, fan clubs, and online communities. Some are very small, with only a handful of subscribers. Some are huge. For example, Win Treese's Internet Index list, internet-index@OpenMarket.com, had 10,118 subscribers as of September 1997.

5.3 Mailing List Programs: Listserv, Listproc, and Majordomo

Perhaps dozens of different mailing list programs are available, but three are most common. Revised List Processor, usually referred to as Listserv, was developed by Eric Thomas and has long been the dominant mailing list program. It has been around since 1986 and recently became a commercial product supported by L-Soft International. Sophisticated and arguably the easiest of the three to use, Listserv became the most popular mailing list program during the heyday of BITNET (Because It's Time Network), a network that catered to academics and researchers who used lists to conduct scholarly discussions.

In the early 1990s, the Internet had clearly surpassed BITNET in both technology and popularity. Many institutions dropped their membership in BITNET and became Internet-only sites. That trend leveled the playing field for list software, and although L-Soft now offers Internet versions of Listserv, several Internet-based programs have since flourished. The most popular, List-processor, or Listproc, was developed by Anastasios Kotsikonas. Its popularity has been bolstered now that it is supported by the Corporation for Research and Educational Networking (CREN). Listproc is similar to Listserv in that it includes a range of features and is easy for subscribers to use.

The third program, called Majordomo, was created by Brent Chapman. It is less commonly used (although gaining popularity), has fewer convenient features, and uses slightly different procedures. Whereas Listserv and Listproc have more features and are designed to handle large volumes of mail, Majordomo is a leaner program that is designed to support smaller lists.

For more information on mailing list software, see these web sites:

Listserv: http://www.lsoft.com/
Listproc: http://www.cren.net/www/listproc/listproc.html
Majordomo: http://www.greatcircle.com/majordomo/

For a frequently asked questions (FAQ) file by Norman Aleks that compares the major mailing list features, send e-mail to **listserv@listserv.net**. Leave the subject line blank, and in the first line type: **GET MLM-SOFT FAQ**.

5.4   Finding Lists

As the number of lists has grown, so has the number of list indexes. These are often referred to as "lists of lists" or "interest groups." Some are simple mailing list addresses, and some include brief descriptions of each list's purpose and subscription procedure. Even with the brief descriptions, though, the best way to discover what a list is like is to subscribe to see what kinds of conversations take place. It's an easy matter to unsubscribe if you find the list does not suit your purposes or address your interests.

Listserv lists

Listserv, as far as we know, is the only mailing list program that is the subject of exclusive list indexes. That is, there are comprehensive indexes of public Listserv lists, but no similar indexes of Listproc or Majordomo lists. Because Listserv is the most commonly used mailing list program, indexes of its lists are generally good resources, especially for finding academically oriented lists. Here's how to find these lists of lists.

Via the Web

>   http://tile.net/lists
>   http://www.liszt.com/

Via e-mail

>   Send e-mail to: listserv@listserv.Net
>   Leave the subject line blank.
>   Write: list global

This shows an entire index of Listserv lists — the document is nearly 7,000 lines long. To narrow the search, you can specify a topic by writing **list global/[topic].**[1] Thus if you wanted to learn about literature lists, you would follow these directions, but you would change **list global** to **list global/literature.**

Interest groups

The term *interest group* refers to indexes of mailing lists and sometimes Usenet newsgroups. These are compiled according to subject, regardless of the software used to support the group. Interest group indexes are sometimes extremely large and often divided into a series of files. Here's where to find some interest groups.

---

1. In all the examples for this chapter, do not type the [ ] that appear in the directions. These indicate a generic category in the command sequence. In this example, it would be the topic of your choice.

Via the Web

http://www.nova.edu/Inter-Links/cgi-bin/news-lists.pl

5.5   Subscribing to Lists

The subscription process is very similar for most mailing list software, but keep in mind that although different programs share functions, they quite often have different ways of accomplishing those functions. Think about the differences between popular word processors like Microsoft Word and WordPerfect. Both have similar functions and features for creating and formatting texts, but each has its own distinct way of doing those things.

> NOTE: One important feature of all mailing list software is that when you send a message to the software, you leave the subject line blank unless you receive specific directions to do otherwise.

This situation illustrates the difference between using networks to communicate with people and using them to communicate with machines. In most cases, when you subscribe, unsubscribe, or change mail settings, you are interacting with mailing list software, not with a human list manager. That means your message has to include very precise information. If one character is missing or out of place, the computer gets confused.

Subscribing in Listserv

Here is the Listserv command protocol.

Command	Comments
Send e-mail to: **listserv@host.domain**	host.domain is the address the list runs on.
Write: **subscribe [listname] Firstname Lastname**	You do not need your e-mail address; that will be read automatically by Listserv. Listserv is not case sensitive.

For example, if John Milton wanted to subscribe to WPA-L, a list for writing program administrators, he would:

Send e-mail to: listserv@asuvm.inre.asu.edu
Write: subscribe wpa-l John Milton

If the list accepts public subscriptions, you'll automatically receive a welcome message with several basic Listserv commands, such as how to unsubscribe from that list. This message includes a suggestion that you keep the note for future reference. We recommend the same. The information may not seem necessary at the time, but when you need to unsubscribe from a list, it is embarrassing to have to ask. Even worse is sending an unsubscribe command to the list itself, which means that everyone on the list gets a copy of a message that only the mailing list program can process. This is a very common error. In fact, it is so common that some list members respond to it with scorn.

Some lists also maintain individualized welcome messages that come in addition to the default message from Listserv. It is a good idea to pay close attention to welcome messages because they often establish the purposes and conventions of the list. When you walk into a roomful of strangers, it's good to have an idea of their general perspective or political leanings; you should know where they're coming from. The same is true for joining a new e-mail list. A little attention at this point may save you some anguish and embarrassment later.

> **HELPFUL HINT:**   Create a folder in your e-mail program for saving all list software messages. If you join a lot of lists, this will keep all the information you need for unsubscribing in one place. This folder will be especially helpful for those times when you will not have access to your e-mail — Christmas break, spring break, summer vacation. You'll find directions for putting list mail on hold until you get back.

Subscribing in Listproc

The procedures for subscribing to and unsubscribing from Listproc lists are identical to those for Listserv lists. The only real difference is in the way you address the note to the mailing list program. Use **listproc@host.domain** rather than **listserv@host.domain**. For example, ACW-L is a list about computers and writing that uses Listproc. To join, John Milton would:

Send e-mail to: listproc@listserv.ttu.edu
Write: subscribe acw-l John Milton

Subscribing in Majordomo

Majordomo is slightly different from Listserv or Listproc in its subscription procedure. Of course, you would use **majordomo@ host.domain** instead of **listserv** or **listproc**. However, in Majordomo, you do not include your name in the subscription command. You may optionally include your e-mail address, but that is not necessary. If you do include your name, Majordomo will put your name into its distribution list *instead* of your address. This will mean you will not get list messages because a message can't be mailed to a name; it must go to an e-mail address.

> Send e-mail to: **majordomo@host.domain**
> Write: **subscribe [listname]**

> or

> Write: **subscribe [listname] [user@host.domain]**

TechNoCulture (TNC) is a Majordomo list. If Jane Austen wanted to subscribe to it, she would:

> Send e-mail to: majordomo@ucet.ufl.edu
> Write: subscribe tnc

> or

> Write: subscribe tnc jane@dead.novelists.com

5.6 Unsubscribing from Lists

Unsubscribing from Listserv

To leave a Listserv list:

> Send e-mail to: **listserv@host.domain**
> Write: **signoff [listname]**

> or

> Write: **unsubscribe [listname]**

Note that unlike the subscribe command, your name is not included. In fact, if you do include your name, the program will be unable to process the command. For example, if John Milton wanted to unsubscribe from WPA-L, he would:

Send e-mail to: listserv@asuvm.inre.asu.edu
Write: signoff wpa-l

On unsubscribing, you will get an automatically generated acknowledgment message, but this one isn't worth saving. It just says you are unsubscribed.

Unsubscribing from Listproc

The procedure is identical to Listserv, but again use **listproc** rather than **listserv** in the address. For John Milton to unsubscribe from ACW-L, he would:

Send e-mail to: listproc@listserv.ttu.edu
Write: signoff acw-l

Unsubscribing from Majordomo

To unsubscribe from Majordomo, the procedure is:

Send e-mail to: **majordomo@host.domain**
Write: **unsubscribe [listname]**

or

Write: **unsubscribe [listname] [user@host.domain]**

For example, if Jane Austen wanted to unsubscribe from TNC, she would:

Send e-mail to: majordomo@ucet.ufl.edu
Write: unsubscribe tnc

or

Write: unsubscribe tnc jane@dead.novelists.com

5.7 Mail Options

Lists can generate great quantities of e-mail. Even lists that are normally docile may go wild on occasion if a particularly controversial subject comes up. The first reaction many people have is acute exasperation. They are often tempted to quickly unsubscribe to stop the relentless tide of mail. However, if you have compelling reasons to stay with a busy list, it's worth learning how to manage the volume.

The simplest and perhaps best approach may be the liberal use of the Delete key. Some people initially feel that deleting messages is rude, an act similar to ignoring someone in face-to-face situations. Of course, no one is likely to know (unless you tell) whether you've deleted any particular message. Besides, it's an accepted practice. Most experienced list subscribers have adapted their reading habits to fit the situation. They "skim and dive," running their eyes quickly over the first part of each note, sometimes getting no further than the subject or sender lines before deciding about whether to read further. They delete often and without hesitation. And it's OK.

Listserv mail options

Several mail options are also available with Listserv. The main options are NOMAIL, MAIL, DIGEST, and INDEX. To use them, you would:

> Send e-mail to: **listserv@host.domain**
> Write: **set [listname] [option]**

NOMAIL tells Listserv to stop the flow of mail but to keep you as a member of the list. MAIL tells Listserv to resume sending mail. A typical use for this command, in addition to taking occasional breaks from the mail flood, is to stop mail during vacations. To set WPA-L to NOMAIL:

> Send e-mail to: listserv@asuvm.inre.asu.edu
> Write: set wpa-l nomail

To begin receiving mail again:

> Write: set wpa-l mail

DIGEST tells Listserv to bundle all the mail for each twenty-four-hour period and send it as a single (often very *big*) message. To change mail delivery to DIGEST:

> Send e-mail to: listserv@asuvm.inre.asu.edu
> Write: set wpa-l digest

To begin receiving mail in non-DIGEST form again:

> Write: set wpa-l nodigest

INDEX tells Listserv to send a single message every day that lists all the notes distributed by the list during the day, along with instructions about how to retrieve only those messages you wish to read. To do this:

Send e-mail to: listserv@asuvm.inre.asu.edu
Write: set wpa-l index

To begin receiving each mail message directly again:

Write: set wpa-l noindex

To see what your current mail settings are on a Listserv list:

Send e-mail to: **listserv@host.domain**
Write: **query [listname]**

To query WPA-L:

Send e-mail to: listserv@asuvm.inre.asu.edu
Write: query wpa-l

Eric's query to WPA-L returned this:

Subscription options for Eric Crump [wleric@SHOWME.MISSOURI. EDU], list WPA-L:

MAIL	You are sent individual postings as they are received
FULLHDR	Full (normal) mail headers (formerly "FULLBSMTP")
REPRO	You receive a copy of your own postings
NOACK	No acknowledgment of successfully processed postings

Had Eric set his subscription to DIGEST or INDEX, those options would have been mentioned in the Listserv response instead of MAIL.

Listproc mail options

Listproc's mail option commands are slightly different from Listserv's. Rather than NOMAIL, Listproc uses POSTPONE. Listproc, like Listserv, has a DIGEST feature, but it does not have an INDEX feature. The protocol for Listproc is to:

Send e-mail to: **listproc@host.domain**
Write: **set [listname] mail [option]**

To POSTPONE mail from ACW-L:

Send e-mail to: listproc@listserv.ttu.edu
Write: set acw-l mail postpone

To resume mail from ACW-L:

Write: set acw-l mail ack

To DIGEST mail from ACW-L:

Send e-mail to: listproc@listserv.ttu.edu
Write: set acw-l mail digest

To return to normal mail delivery:

Write: set acw-l mail ack

To check your current mail settings on a Listproc list:

Send e-mail to: **listproc@host.domain**
Write: **set [listname]**

Notice that the word *mail* is not needed as part of the command structure. To run this command for ACW-L:

Send e-mail to: listproc@listserv.ttu.edu
Write: set acw-l

Here's what Eric's subscription on ACW-L sent back after he checked his mail settings:

Current settings are:
ADDRESS = WLERIC@SHOWME.MISSOURI.EDU
MAIL = ACK
PASSWORD = xxxxxxxx
CONCEAL = NO

Majordomo mail options

Majordomo does not currently support all the mail options offered by Listserv and Listproc.

5.8 Archives

The majority of public lists are archived, meaning a copy of each note is stored somewhere, usually on the same computer where the list resides. It can be important to know if a list is archived and how to access the archive files. Since most students have limited storage space on their e-mail accounts, it's not practical to save every note that might come in handy some day — especially when those notes are already being stored elsewhere.

Listserv archives

To see if Listserv lists are archived:

> Send e-mail to: **listserv@host.domain**
> Write: **index [listname]**

If no archive exists for the list, Listserv returns a brief note saying the index file is not known. The command **index wcentr-1** returned the following message:

```
File 'WCENTR-L FILELIST' is unknown to LISTSERV
```

If we wanted to see whether WPA-L was archived, we would send mail to listserv@asuvm.inre.asu.edu with the command **index wpa-l.**

The resulting note indicates that WPA-L is archived and that the files are compiled monthly. An excerpt from the reply Listserv sent about WPA-L follows. It shows the files for early 1993. In the excerpt you see a list of "logs," files that contain all the messages written in the week indicated by the "Started on" date.

```
*
* NOTEBOOK archives for the list
* (Monthly notebook)
*                         rec     last - change
* filename filetype   GET PUT -fm lrecl nrecs   date    time  Remarks
* ----------- ----------- --- ---- ---- ------ ------- ------------ ---------------
  WPA-L   LOG9301   ALL OWN V   80  447 93/01/31 14:31:03
Started on Sun, 10 Jan 1993 18:13:00 CST
  WPA-L   LOG9302   ALL OWN V   86  4677 93/02/27 22:26:34
Started on Mon, 1 Feb 1993 09:28:32 -0700
  WPA-L   LOG9303   ALL OWN V   80  2995 93/03/30 14:19:04
Started on Mon, 1 Mar 1993 12:34:35 -0800
  WPA-L   LOG9304   ALL OWN V   80  3332 93/04/30 12:03:24
Started on Mon, 5 Apr 1993 10:46:19 -0700
  WPA-L   LOG9305   ALL OWN V   80  3478 93/05/30 15:53:54
Started on Sat, 1 May 1993 18:45:29 -0700
```

Each of the files can be obtained from Listserv using the **get** command. For instance, to get the file from February:

> Send e-mail to: listserv@asuvm.inre.asu.edu
> Write: get wpa-l log9302

Listproc archives

The **index** command also works to determine whether a Listproc list is archived. Here's how the command would be used for ACW-L:

> Send e-mail to: listproc@listserv.ttu.edu
> Write: index acw-l

Here's part of the reply from Listproc:

> Archive: acw-l (path: acw-l) -- Files:
> 9504 (1 part, 1064767 bytes)
> 9505 (1 part, 567640 bytes)
> 9506 (1 part, 704249 bytes)
> 9507 (1 part, 354450 bytes)
> 9508 (1 part, 428490 bytes)
> 9509 (1 part, 757397 bytes)

This message tells you the path on TTU's system where the files are located, but that is not something you need remember. It also lets you know that the files are collected monthly (9504 refers to April 1995, 9506 to June 1995, and so on). And it tells you how large each file is. The file for May 1995 is more than 567K, for example. To get the file for April, you would send another message to Listproc (using the same address shown earlier), including the command **get acw-l acw-l.log9504.**

ACW-L, like many lists these days, also has web-based archives available. See http://www.ttu.edu/lists/acw-l/ as an example.

Majordomo archives

The index command produces the same basic results with Majordomo lists, but the message has a different look. For example:

> Send e-mail to: majordomo@ucet.ufl.edu
> Write: index tnc

The response looks like this:

```
>>>> index tnc
total 152
-rw-rw-r-- 1 daemon   majordom   77299 Jun 27 00:26 archive
```

The filename, archive, is at the end of the last line. The total indicates the number of messages in the file (152) and -rw-rw-r-- shows the file attributes. You also learn that it is a Majordomo file of 77299 bytes and that it was last updated on June 27 at twenty-six minutes after noon.

To retrieve the archive file:

Send e-mail to: majordomo@ucet.ufl.edu
Write: get tnc archive

Web and gopher archives

Mailing list archives can be made available via the Web or gopher (a menu-based, text-only program), as well as via e-mail. Web archives are especially convenient to use since they are easy to search and sort.

5.9 Common Problems

Mailing list software is powerful, whether you're using the sophisticated Listserv or the simpler Majordomo, but it is also stupid. New users can often become frustrated because they believe they are following procedures exactly, but the list software refuses to understand their commands. Like most commonly used software, mailing list programs are capable of responding to precise commands only. Anything even slightly different is completely unrecognizable.

One wrong character

Computer screens can be difficult to read, especially when you are trying to distinguish between similar-looking characters. For example, it's not unusual for people to mistake lowercase Ls for the numeral one, and because many list names end in L, this confusion leads to a good deal of frustration. If you get an error message from Listserv or Listproc or Majordomo suggesting that the list you refer to does not exist, one thing to check is whether you've got your ls and 1s straight.

Right syntax, wrong program

Although the differences between mailing list programs are generally slight, those slight differences might as well be vast chasms when it comes to software "comprehension." Speak Listservese to Listproc, and the program will stare at you blankly. When in doubt about the exact command syntax, send a one-word command to Listproc (or Listserv or Majordomo): help. The basic help message includes instructions on how to get help files on specific commands.

Talking to the wrong people

One of the most common errors made on the Net is posting mailing list commands to lists. That is, messages that are meant for the software to process are sent to the people who are subscribed to the list. With the exception of the list owner, there's nothing those people can do with the command — except get annoyed at the person who sent it for cluttering their mail in-boxes with junk. Always remember to address commands to the software — Listserv, Listproc, Majordomo, or whatever program you're trying to communicate with — not to the list.

Unintentional masquerading

This problem is rarely caused by users and can usually be fixed by contacting list owners. When you subscribe to lists, the software picks up your address from the header of the subscription message. The mailing list uses that address to identify you as a subscriber. If you send a message from another address, even a very similar one, the program cannot recognize you as being you. Being off by one character or word is all it takes. Even though the addresses may look as though they belong to the same person, from the mailing list's perspective, geoff.chaucer@canterbury.edu is an entirely different user from geoff.chaucer@miller.canterbury.edu.

5.10 Getting Help

Before you get to the point of utter frustration with a list-related problem, contact the list owner and ask for assistance. Nearly all list owners are volunteers. They start and maintain lists because they think the venue provides a service to a specific community of people with interests similar to theirs. Part of their responsibility is to help people who run into problems subscribing, signing off, or changing subscription settings.

Like any frustrating situation, it's tempting to get some of that anger and anxiety off your chest. Be careful, though, not to direct your frustration at the person who's in a position to help you. List owners, for instance, are often as frustrated as subscribers by the strange and inscrutable problems that pop up on the Net. They are your allies, not your opponents. They can often help you quickly solve a problem. Try to explain in as much detail as you can exactly what you tried to do and what the result was. It's always a good idea to write down any error messages you receive. Even if they make no sense to you, they might make sense to someone with more experience, and help him or her deduce the solution.

To find the e-mail address of a Listserv list owner:

Send e-mail to: **listserv@host.domain**
Write: **review [listname] short**

For WPA-L:

Send e-mail to: listserv@asuvm.inre.asu.edu
Write: review wpa-l short

You will receive a file of information about the list, including the owner information. Here's the excerpt of how this information appears for WPA-L. Notice that the owner is clearly identified:

```
*
* Writing Program Administration
*
* Review= Public   Subscription= Open,Confirm Send= Public
* Confirm-Delay= 72 h
* Notify= Yes   Reply to= List,Ignore   Files= No
* CONFIDENTIAL= YES   VALIDATE= STORE ONLY
* X-Tags= Yes   Stats= Normal,Owners   Ack= Msg
* NOTEBOOK= YES,E,MONTHLY,PUBLIC
* ERRORS-TO= OWNER
* DIGEST= YES,SAME,DAILY,24
* Owner= IACDES@ASUACAD (David Schwalm)
```

To find the owner of a Listproc list:

Send e-mail to: **listproc@host.domain**
Write: **review [listname]**

For ACW-L:

Send e-mail to: listproc@listserv.ttu.edu
Write: review acw-l

When you get your reply, look for the address in the cc: line of the header that comes at the top of the message sent to you by Listproc:

From: listproc@ttacs6.ttu.edu
To: wleric@showme.missouri.edu
Cc: ejand@ttacs6.ttu.edu
Subject: REVIEW ACW-L

Any queries you need to make to the owner of ACW-L can be addressed to nobody@listserv.ttu.edu.

To find the appropriate address for a Majordomo list:

Send e-mail to: **majordomo@host.domain**
Write: **info [listname]**

For TNC (TechNoCulture):

Send e-mail to: majordomo@ucet.ufl.edu
Write: info tnc

As part of the reply, you will find this:

If you have problems using Majordomo, or if you need help on a matter unrelated to the mailing lists, please direct your questions to "system@ucet.ufl.edu".

6

Telnetting on the Internet

6.1 Introduction

Telnet is the protocol used to connect your computer to another on the Internet. You are most likely to use it in one of two ways. You have to log into your Internet account and, at the account prompt, type the command **telnet** and an address. Or you have to have access to a computer on campus that has a dedicated telnet connection. (A dedicated connection is a cable connection between your computer and the host computer.) With these you can choose a telnet icon from your desktop; you will then receive a dialog box asking you to type in the domain address you wish to reach.

Once you reach the other computer by telnet, you may have to log into it. A few telnet addresses will connect you to an automatic login; others will give you the login name and password; and still others will require you to know in advance the login name and password to use.

HELPFUL HINT: Telnet is useful for reaching your own account when you are away from your campus. If you visit a friend at another school, you can access your computer through your friend's. After he or she logs on, telnet to your campus computer. When you are prompted for a login and password, use the same ones you use at your campus. For this to work, you need to know the telnet address for your campus.

40

6.2   Connecting to a Telnet Database

The best way to understand telnet is to think of it as *tele*phoning on the Inter*net*. In the following example, you will dial Harvard's Online Library Information Service (HOLLIS) to access the Educational Resources Information Center (ERIC) database.

At the prompt (in this example, prompt%) type:

prompt%**telnet 128.103.151.247 3006**

where:

> **telnet** = the command — typing it is akin to picking up a phone receiver and poising your fingers over the numbers; note the command is in lowercase.
> **128.103.151.247** = the number you want to connect to — it's the Internet number for Harvard's library
> **3006** = the extension (or port) for the ERIC database

Note that there is no space between the prompt and the start of the command. You must have a space between telnet and the number, as well as between the address number and the extension you are trying to reach. Further, since this example takes place in a UNIX operating system, the command is typed in lowercase.

Because you are working from a prompt line and not a menu system, you will need to hit the Enter key after each command.

After a few moments, the following appears:

Trying
Connected to 128.103.151.247.
Escape character is ^.

HOLLIS Plus
Now connecting to HOLLIS

To leave this resource hold down the control key (Ctrl) and press x.
(^X)

This information scrolls by with only a short pause. The screen shown in Figure 6.1 then appears.

```
oit
ER SEARCH OPTIONS
                              ERIC

                           Produced by
          the Educational Resources Information Center

To begin a search, select a search option from the list below and type its
code on the COMMAND line. Use either upper or lower case.
To begin a search, type:        AU        Author search
                                TI        Title search
                                SU        Subject search
                                ON        ERIC accession number search

To see more options, type:      KEYWORD   Keyword search options

For information on the contents of ERIC, type HELP.
To exit ERIC, type QUIT

A search can be entered on the COMMAND line of any screen.

      ALWAYS PRESS THE ENTER OR RETURN KEY AFTER TYPING YOUR COMMAND.
COMMAND?
```

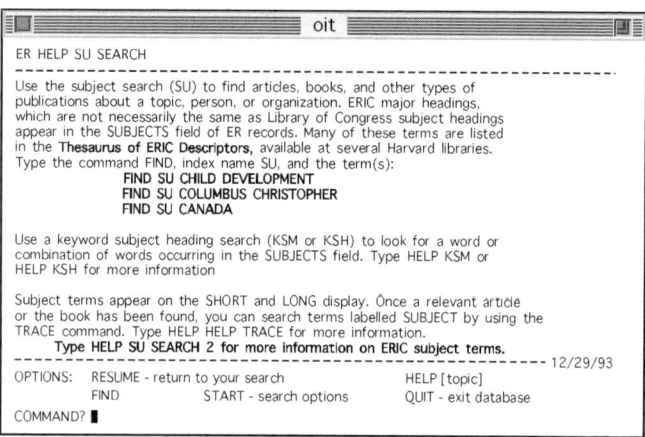

Figure 6.1

Typing **su**, a command you are sending from your keyboard through the telnet connection to HOLLIS, gets you to the screen shown in Figure 6.2.

```
oit
ER HELP SU SEARCH
--------------------------------------------------------------------
Use the subject search (SU) to find articles, books, and other types of
publications about a topic, person, or organization. ERIC major headings,
which are not necessarily the same as Library of Congress subject headings
appear in the SUBJECTS field of ER records. Many of these terms are listed
in the Thesaurus of ERIC Descriptors, available at several Harvard libraries.
Type the command FIND, index name SU, and the term(s):
                FIND SU CHILD DEVELOPMENT
                FIND SU COLUMBUS CHRISTOPHER
                FIND SU CANADA

Use a keyword subject heading search (KSM or KSH) to look for a word or
combination of words occurring in the SUBJECTS field. Type HELP KSM or
HELP KSH for more information

Subject terms appear on the SHORT and LONG display. Once a relevant article
or the book has been found, you can search terms labelled SUBJECT by using the
TRACE command. Type HELP HELP TRACE for more information.
     Type HELP SU SEARCH 2 for more information on ERIC subject terms.
-------------------------------------------------------------- 12/29/93
OPTIONS:  RESUME - return to your search              HELP [topic]
          FIND             START - search options     QUIT - exit database
COMMAND? ▮
```

Figure 6.2

The command **su shakespeare** gives the result shown in Figure 6.3.

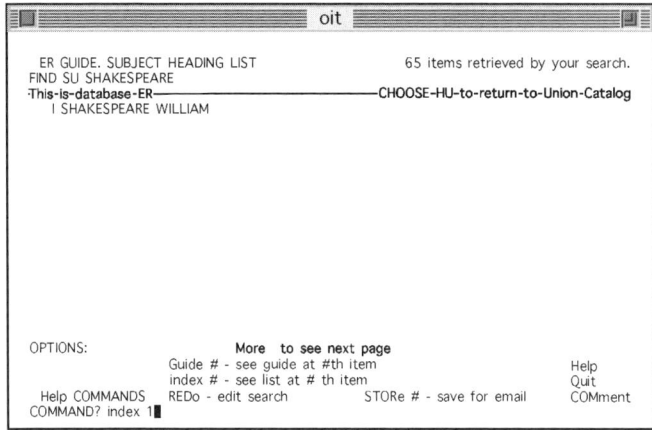

Figure 6.3

As you can see from the sequence of screen snapshots, the telnet interface is text only. In this example, you connected directly to an online database. The commands you typed at the computer activated a program stored at Harvard's library. With a little practice, you can become comfortable using telnet in a number of different interfaces. The important thing to remember is that while in telnet your keyboard is sending commands to a distant computer. To see another example of a telnet session, go to Chapters 10 and 11.

HELPFUL HINT: Because you are sending a signal over a longer distance, you will sometimes experience lag time while using telnet. Lag time means that you have to wait a bit for your signal to reach the computer and for the computer to send the signal back to your screen. Lag time can be aggravated by telnetting at peak hours (8 a.m. to 5 p.m., Monday through Friday) or if the host computer (the computer you reach) or application is being heavily used.

7

File Transfer Protocol

CHAPTER CONTENTS

7.1 Introduction

7.2 Anonymous FTP

7.3 A Brief Look at Fetch

7.1 Introduction

File transfer protocol (FTP) is an Internet procedure used to get a file from a remote computer on the Internet and have it sent to the computer from which you issue the FTP command. If you connect to your Internet account with a modem to a server and type the FTP command at the prompt, the transferred file will be saved to your account space on the server. To move the file to the computer on your disk is another step. If you have a direct access or PPP/SLIP (point-to-point protocol/serial line Internet protocol) connection that allows you to use an automated FTP program such as Fetch, the file will be placed directly onto your personal computer.

7.2 Anonymous FTP

A number of Internet computers host anonymous FTP sites. Anonymous FTP allows outside users to log in as a guest and retrieve files stored on the host's computer. Since accessing these files is akin to someone leaving the backdoor unlocked and the porch light on, it is courteous to keep the following in mind:

1. If possible, FTP at a time when the host machine is not likely to be busy.
2. As a login name, use the word *anonymous*.
3. When asked for a password or identification, type in your e-mail address. This allows the site managers to have a sense of where users are coming from. Of course, it ceases

to make you anonymous in the strict sense of the word. Anonymous in this sense does not mean privacy; it's like having a guest pass.

The following example — an FTP session to the University of Kansas public FTP archives to retrieve a copy of Lynx — is based on using a UNIX platform reached by dialing in from a modem. Note that the commands are written in lowercase because UNIX is a case-sensitive operating system. In this example, prompt% is the name of the starting system's UNIX server; commands entered are in bold; explanatory notes are in roman.

The example features the use of the following commands:

ftp [address]	Initiates an FTP connection from a command line prompt.
anonymous	The username for logging into publicly available archives.
ls or dir	Lists files and other directories in the current directory of an FTP server.
cd [directory name]	Changes directories into the named directory.
cdup	Changes up to a previous directory. This makes sense as a concept if you think of each directory you enter as moving you farther down a directory tree.
get [filename]	Transfer a file to the computer from which you began the FTP session.
quit	Ends an FTP session; this will close the connection and return you to your own command line prompt.

prompt%ftp **ftp2.cc.ukans.edu**
Trying 129.237.33.1

Connected to ukanaix.cc.ukans.edu.
220 ukanaix.cc.ukans.edu FTP server
(Version 4.9 Thu Sep 2 20:35:07 CDT 1993) ready.
Name (FTP2.cc.ukans.edu:nickc): **anonymous**
331 Guest login ok, send ident as password.

Password:

When you type the password, you will not see the letters on your screen. This is a security feature of computer passwords used to keep people from learning your password by looking over your shoulder.

230 Guest login ok, access restrictions apply.

After completing the login, a prompt appears. The next series of commands are used to navigate the FTP directories at the site.

FTP> ls

This command lists files and directories. Note that the screen gives a lot of information, including that the command succeeded.

200 PORT command successful.

This indicates the **ls** command was received and is in progress.

150 Opening data connection for /bin/ls.

This indicates the data for the command will be accessed.

bin
etc
lib
pub
usr
226 Transfer complete.
25 bytes received in 0.0039 second (6.3 Kbytes/s)

These are the names of directories you can access, followed by a progress message. The number may not mean much to most of us, but the words tell us that the command worked.

FTP> cd pub/WWW/lynx

The **cd** command stands for change directory. In the example, we move three directories at once, into pub, into WWW (a directory within the pub directory), and then into Lynx (a directory within the WWW directory). We could move one directory at a time as well. The first time you visit a site, you may want to just learn your way around. Unless you have directions indicating otherwise, most visits to an FTP site will begin with the pub, for public access, directory. After completing the command, the following message appears:

250 CWD command successful.

FTP>**ls**

While in the pub/WWW/Lynx directory, the **ls** command reveals the files and folders listed. Files will often have extensions (such as tar.Z) that indicate the compression format used to make the file take up less space on the disk; however, often does not mean always (note the file called README below).

200 PORT command successful.
150 Opening data connection for /bin/ls.
README
freeWAIS-0.202.tar.Z
Lynx2-2
Lynx2-3
Lynx2-3-7
Lynx2-4
Lynx2-4-1
Lynx2html.tar.Z
Lynx_help_files.tar.Z
Lynx_help_files.zip
mailcap
mime.types
226 Transfer complete.
161 bytes received in 0.0039 second (40 Kbytes/s)

FTP> cd Lynx2-4-1

250 CWD command successful.

You can see that all names have file compression format extensions. (To save space, archives are compressed by special software that cuts down the file's number of bytes.) Instead of typing **cd Lynx2-4-1** as shown, we first tried **get Lynx2-4-1** and received a message that Lynx2-4-1 was not a file, but a directory. We mention this because you will likely make the same mistake at some point. When you do, just know that instead of **get**, you will want to use **cd**.

```
FTP> ls

200 PORT command successful.
150 Opening data connection for /bin/ls.
Lynx2-4-1.aix32.exe.Z
Lynx2-4-1.linux-ncurses.exe.Z
Lynx2-4-1.osf.exe.Z
Lynx2-4-1.tar.Z
Lynx2-4-1.zip
226 Transfer complete.
107 bytes received in 0.0078 seconds (13 Kbytes/s)
FTP> get Lynx2-4-1.zip
```

The **get** command is used to actually transfer the file to the computer from which the FTP session was launched. It is important to type the filename exactly as it appears in the directory listing.

```
200 PORT command successful.
150 Opening data connection for Lynx2-4-1.zip (727242 bytes).
226 Transfer complete.
local: Lynx2-4-1.zip remote: Lynx2-4-1.zip
729978 bytes received in 1.302 seconds (5.4 Kbytes/s)

FTP> cdup
```

The **cdup** command moves you back one directory at a time. We need to use it in this example to go back to the directory where the Lynx help files are stored.

```
250 CWD command successful.
FTP> get Lynx_help_files.zip
```

200 PORT command successful.
150 Opening data connection for Lynx_help_files.zip (57449 bytes).
226 Transfer complete.
local: Lynx_help_files.zip remote: Lynx_help_files.zip
57654 bytes received in 7.4 seconds (7.6 Kbytes/s)

FTP> **quit**

221 Goodbye.

Since these files are compacted with zip compression software, all we need to do in this case is unzip them. (Zip software specializes in archiving. A "zipped" file uses half the space as an unzipped file.) Back on our own computer, we type the command to unzip the files. Of course, before you can do this, you need to make sure the computer you use has the unzip software. As you see in the next command line, you type the command name followed by the name of the file. After you do this, you will see a list of separate files. Compression software can also take many files and put them into one file for easier transfer among computers.

prompt%unzip Lynx2-4-1.zip

After completing this command, you will find a number of files to use in setting up Lynx, including directions. However, before installing any software on your account, check to see if you need it (Lynx may already be available) and if you have permission to install it on the server. See Chapter 8 for a full example of how to unzip a file.

7.3 A Brief Look at Fetch

Fetch, a Macintosh program for making FTP connections, works via a PPP/SLIP connection to "fetch" programs and files from remote computers and download them. If you have a decompression program, such as StuffIt Expander, Fetch can activate the decompression utility. Thus with Fetch you can download and decompress software very quickly.

Fetch can be set to automatically tell if a file to be downloaded is binary or text. Fetch can also be used to upload files from your computer to your user account. For example, if you are creating a hypertext essay on UNIX, Fetch can upload your images and text files in bulk.

Figure 7.1 shows a screen snapshot of Fetch's dialog box as it appears when you first open it. You will notice that each box asks for parts of the FTP process. The host in this example is ftp. dartmouth.edu. Dartmouth is the home of Fetch and where you can FTP to for a copy. The connection in the example was by anonymous FTP; therefore the password used was Nick's e-mail address. The directory chosen was pub. You could type in the full directory path to the files if you know it. If you have a site you will be returning to often, you can set up all the information needed and save it as one of your shortcuts. Shortcuts in Fetch work the same way bookmarks do in Netscape. If you were going to place items in your own account space, you would use your home host, your user id, your password, and if you'd like, the path in your account space where you want the files to be placed.

Figure 7.2 shows Fetch in action, after a connection has been made, downloading *Tarzan of the Apes* — an item from Dartmouth's Hyperbook collection.

Once a connection is made, Fetch creates a separate window for files from the FTP site. To choose a file, double-click on it

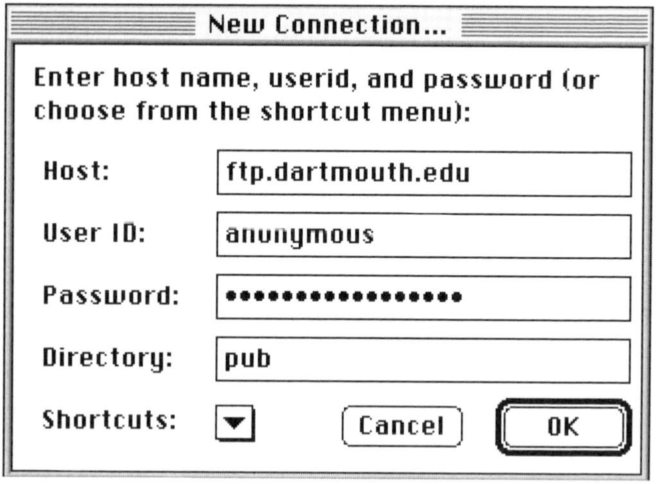

Figure 7.1

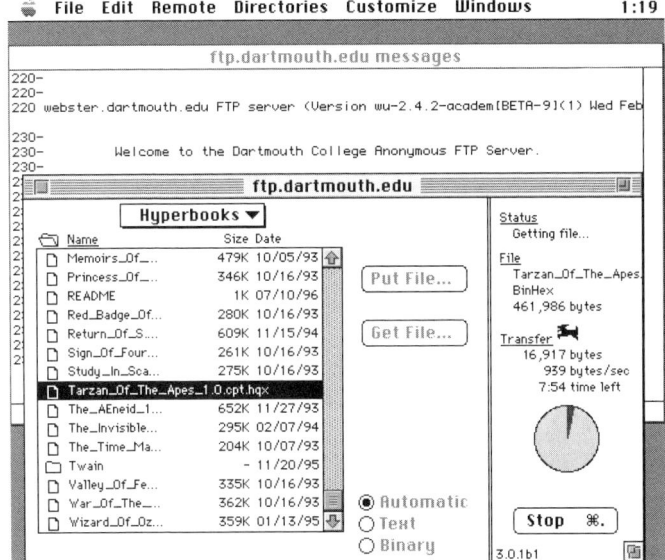

Figure 7.2

with your mouse. The drop box above the scroll bar window where you view the files says Hyperbooks. If you click on the down arrow, you'll see a list of directories for Hyperbooks. This feature gives you a history of your path and allows you to move back one or more directories (similar to what **cdup** does in standard FTP interfaces).

If you have a connection — MacTCP, PPP, or SLIP — that allows you to use Fetch, get it. Fetch is copyrighted by the Trustees of Dartmouth College and is licensed freely to those affiliated with educational or nonprofit organizations. You can learn more at   http://www.dartmouth.edu/pages/softdev/fetch.html.   Once you've downloaded and installed Fetch, you'll discover its excellent help menu, including an FTP tutorial.

Remember that Fetch is a Macintosh program. To find an FTP program for Windows, go to http://www.shareware.com/, select your version of Windows (3.1, 95, or NT), and for a search term use FTP. One final note, both Netscape and Internet Explorer can do FTP downloads.

8

Getting Freeware and Shareware from Public Archives

8.1 Introduction

One of the features of the Internet that may surprise new users is its overriding spirit of cooperation. One example of this is the software programs developed by individuals and businesses that are stored in archives anyone can access. Users can browse the archives and select the software they'd like to try.

The archives are usually provided by universities that have significant storage space. The archives contain all manner of software, including various utility programs, games, educational programs, and communications programs.

8.2 Freeware

Software labeled freeware is simply there for the taking. An example of freeware is Disinfectant, a Macintosh antivirus program created by John Norstad. He and his colleagues not only make the program available free of charge, but every time a new Macintosh virus appears, they quickly revise the program to account for the new threat. They very often release a new version of Disinfectant within a few days of the discovery of a new virus.

> HELPFUL HINT: You should make sure you have up-to-date virus detection software on your computer. Viruses are programs that wreak havoc in computers. Sometimes they are casual pranks, but other times they are highly destructive. Use protection software whenever you download an Internet file from an archive.

8.3   Shareware

Software labeled shareware comes with a price, almost always a modest price, and can be downloaded by anyone. No bills or invoices arrive by postal mail, however. Each transaction is based on the honor system. If you download a shareware program and like it enough to keep using it, you're expected to send the author his or her asking price, which is usually between $5 and $25 per copy. Shareware programs sometimes come with just the address of the developer, which may be displayed during the program's startup process. Or they may come with a registration form ready to print and mail in.

8.4   Downloading

Most archives are stored on machines running UNIX systems, and they are tapped by using file transfer protocol (FTP). You can also reach software archives through gopher or the World Wide Web. One excellent WWW resource is http://www.shareware. com/ a page that allows users to search several archives at once.

When accessing software, you will notice that it is compressed so that it does not take up as much space and downloads faster. Since a compressed file often contains more than one file, it helps to think of it as a packed suitcase. Decompressing unpacks the suitcase and lets you use what's inside. When shareware and freeware are stored in archives, they are put into individual files by compression software that encodes and packs them. By packing many files and lots of data into one suitcase, it becomes easier for the software to travel.

However, this means that you will need some way to decompress the software before you can use it. If you are lucky, you have access that will automate the decompression for you. The exact procedure for downloading and unpacking software to a personal computer can vary quite a bit depending on the capabilities of your system.

8.5   Macintosh Decompression Utilities

Once a freeware or shareware file is on your machine, you need to run decompression and decoding utilities to render it ready to use. Those utilities are often available from college computing services departments, or they can be purchased. Many archived programs are now compressed in "self-extracting archives" (noted by the use of .sea as the extension after the filename). Those files do not require any additional utility programs in order to decompress and decode them. However, you would do well to get a good decompression software program. One very good one, available for both Macintosh and PC formats, is StuffIt Expander, from Aladdin Systems (http://www.aladdinsys.com/).

As the folks at Aladdin note on the homepage for StuffIt, one of the problems with downloading decompression software for Macintoshes is that you need decompression software to decompress the decompression software. Chicken and egg indeed! StuffIt Expander is Aladdin's Freeware software for expanding files compressed for the Macintosh. It can expand StuffIt files (.sit), BinHex files (.hqx), MacBinary files (.bin), and Compact Pro files (.cpt). Because you need software to unpack the software, the URL http://www.aladdinsys.com/obstufex.htm gives you details on a number of ways to solve this problem, including checking online services such as America Online. If none of the suggestions look as though they will work for you, you can query Aladdin by e-mail at cust.service@aladdinsys.com. In your subject heading, you should write Query Freeware StuffIt Expander. In your e-mail, explain that you are interested in a copy of their freeware version of StuffIt Expander, but cannot access a decompressed copy. They'll let you know how to order an unpacked version for the cost of a diskette and shipping and handling.

8.6 Windows Decompression Utilities

Aladdin also makes a version of StuffIt that will run on Windows. If you go to URL http://www.aladdinsys.com/#SFP, you'll find a link to the version for Windows. It comes as a Windows executable file. (Executable files use an .exe extension and are used for running programs.) All you have to do is download it to your computer, and it is ready to run. Make sure you set your communications software to download the file as binary and not text. Follow the directions in Windows for adding new software, and you'll be all set to go. StuffIt Expander for Windows will decompress the following file types: StuffIt (.sit), ZIP (.zip), uuencoded (.uue), BinHex (.hqx), MacBinary (.bin), ARC (.arc), Arj (.arj), and gzip (.gz).

> **HELPFUL HINT:** The Windows version will decompress Macintosh formats. With newer model Power Macintoshes, disks formatted for PCs can be read by Macs. If you have a friend with Windows, and you use Macintosh, you can download StuffIt Expander on Windows, set it up, and then use that to decompress StuffIt Expander for your Macintosh.

8.7 Common Sites for Freeware and Shareware

Macintosh and INFO-Mac software archives

Because of the persistently heavy load on Stanford's INFO-Mac archive, its maintainers recommend that people try to use nearby "mirrors" of their site instead. The original FTP site apparently is no longer accessible, in fact, so the homepage on the Web (http://www.pht.com/info-mac/) may be the best starting point for INFO-Mac information and links to mirror sites. The mirror sites, like a mirror image, contain identical copies of the files located at the Stanford University INFO-Mac home site. Some of the sites in the United States that mirror Stanford University's INFO-Mac archives follow.

INFO-Mac mirrors

UUNET Technologies, Falls Church, Virginia
FTP://FTP.uu.net/systems/mac/info-mac

University of Hawaii, Honolulu, Hawaii
FTP://FTP.hawaii.edu/mirrors/info-mac/

University of Illinois at Urbana-Champaign, Urbana, Illinois
FTP://uiarchive.cso.uiuc.edu/pub/systems/mac/info-mac/
http://uiarchive.cso.uiuc.edu/

University of Iowa, Iowa City, Iowa
Telnet://grind.isca.uiowa.edu/mac/infomac/
FTP://grind.isca.uiowa.edu/mac/infomac/

MIT Laboratory for Computer Science, Cambridge, Massachusetts
http://hyperarchive.lcs.mit.edu/HyperArchive.html

Washington University, St. Louis, Missouri
FTP://wuarchive.wustl.edu/systems/mac/info-mac/
http://wuarchive.wustl.edu/systems/mac/info-mac/
Gopher://wuarchive.wustl.edu/11/systems/mac/info-mac/
fsp://wuarchive.wustl.edu/systems/mac/info-mac/
nfs://wuarchive.wustl.edu/archive/systems/mac/info-mac/

The GLOBE at Cornell University, Ithaca, New York
http://globe1.csuglab.cornell.edu/

Oregon State University, Corvallis, Oregon
FTP://FTP.orst.edu/pub/systems/info-mac/

University of Michigan, Ann Arbor, Michigan
http://www.umich.edu/~archive/mac/

Windows and DOS software archives

California State University-San Marcos, San Marcos, California
http://coyote.csusm.edu/cwis/winworld/winworld.html

Greater Flint Educational Consortium
(TUCOWS: The Ultimate Collection of Winsock Software)
http://GFECnet.gmi.edu/Software/

Windows and DOS software mirrors

Northern Indiana Internet Access, Inc.
http://www.niia.Net/tucows/

Solar Eclipse Information Services
  http://www.seis.com/~tucows/

The Genesee Free-Net
  http://gfn1.genesee.freenet.org/tucows/

OAK Software Repository (Oakland University)
  http://www.acs.oakland.edu/oak/oak.html

For more Mac and PC shareware sites, see Jim Knopf's Father of Shareware web page at: http://www.halcyon.com/knopf/jim.

8.8 How to FTP Freeware and Shareware for Macs and PCs

If you prefer to access freeware and shareware written for Macintosh or PC operating systems by FTP instead of using a gopher or WWW access, and if you do not have a connection enabling you to use an automated program such as Fetch, then the following FTP examples will be helpful. In Chapter 7, we showed you the basics of FTP. In that chapter, we used an example where we got a copy of a UNIX-based program; we FTPed from a UNIX workstation, and everything was straightforward. The examples in this section have a few wrinkles you need to know about when you FTP for software to use on your own computer.

The following example shows what the Washington University archives would look like if you were looking for Macintosh freeware and shareware. WU's archive contains mirrors of a number of big FTP sites. The archive itself is one of the most popular and most important FTP servers on the Internet.

HELPFUL HINT: Many FTP servers provide a welcome message or message of the day (MOD). These messages sometimes contain important information about using the site, so it's worth giving them a glance.

prompt> **ftp wuarchive.wustl.edu**
Connected to wuarchive.wustl.edu.
220 wuarchive.wustl.edu FTP server (Version wu-2.4(3) Tue Aug 8 15:35:34
CDT 1995) r.

Name (wuarchive.wustl.edu:wleric): **anonymous**
331 Guest login ok, send your complete e-mail address as password.
Password:

230- If your FTP client crashes or hangs shortly after login please try
230- using a dash (-) as the first character of your password. This will
230- turn off the informational messages that may be confusing
230- your FTP client.
230- This system may be used 24 hours a day, 7 days a week. The
230- local time is Wed Aug 30 23:12:56 1995. You are user number
230- 299 out of a possible 300. All transfers to and from wuarchive
230- are logged. If you don't like this then disconnect now!
230 Guest login ok, access restrictions apply.

Failed connection messages

Many software archives are popular spots, but the machines they
reside on do not have limitless capacity for simultaneous logins.
Usually when you try to login as "anonymous" and the connection fails, it's because the machine is too busy to handle any
more users. Here is what the Washington University FTP server's
too-busy message looks like:

Name (wuarchive.wustl.edu:wleric): **anonymous**
530- Sorry, there are too many anonymous FTP users using the
530- system at this time. Please try again in a few minutes.
530-
530- There is currently a limit of 300 anonymous users. Yes, there
530- REALLY are that many users on wuarchive — this message is not
530 the result of a bug. User anonymous access denied.
Login failed.

If the FTP server is busy, it rejects the anonymous login right
away and doesn't waste your time requesting your e-mail address
as a password.

Getting software files

If you're using a UNIX or other general-use system like VM/CMS
(Virtual Machine/Conversational Monitor System) or VMS (Digital Equipment Corporation's operating system), you will need to

change the file type to binary, and then type the command **get** followed by the exact filename as it appears in the directory. You do this by typing an **i** before you type **get**. This step is crucial for downloading from a UNIX, VM/CMS, or VMS workstation to either a Macintosh or PC. Here is an example of changing directories and getting a file, in this case, to get to the INFO-Mac archive directory to access virus detection software. We take you through the steps of changing directories and finding the file wanted. Note that the command to change the file to binary is used just before issuing the **get** command. The purpose is to make sure both systems agree on the file type. Remember, binary files are programs, images, audio, and formatted text files.

You've logged in and got your bearings at the Washington University FTP server, and now you are ready to go to their INFO-Mac archives.

FTP> cd info-mac
250 CWD command successful.

FTP> dir

The **dir** command is an alternative to **ls**. Not all servers will support both; you may have to try one or the other. Like **ls, dir** will list everything in the directory.

200 PORT command successful.
150 Opening ASCII mode data connection for /bin/ls.
total 143
lrwxrwxrwx 1   root   archive   22 Mar 8 23:29 00readme.txt
                                  ->help/about-art
drwxr-xr-x 26 root   archive   1024 Jun 6 02:48 Old
lrwxrwxrwx 1   root   archive   3 May 23 23:16 _Anti-Virus -> vir
lrwxrwxrwx 1   root   archive   3 May 23 23:16 _Application -> app
lrwxrwxrwx 1   root   archive   3 May 30 00:03 _Art_&_Info -> art

For brevity's sake, we have deleted the middle portion of this list — it takes up nearly a page.

drwxr-xr-x   2   root   archive   12288 Aug 21 04:55 rec
drwxr-xr-x   2   root   archive   9728 Aug 21 04:55 sci
drwxr-xr-x   3   root   archive   11264 Aug 20 03:47 snd

```
drwxr-xr-x  4  root archive  8192 Aug 20 03:38 text
drwxr-xr-x  2  root archive  1024 Aug 20 03:46 vir
226 Transfer complete.
```

```
FTP> cd vir
250 CWD command successful.
```

You can tell this is a directory you can go into because the line begins with drwxr-xr-x. The initial d in the string is the directory indicator.

```
FTP> dir
200 PORT command successful.
150 Opening ASCII mode data connection for /bin/ls.
total 997
-rw-r—r— 1 root wheel 214490 Apr 7 21:38 distinfectant-36.hqx
-r—r—r— 1 root archive 322288 Nov 13 1993 gatekeeper-130.hqx
```

Once again, many files were listed. We've deleted from this example about thirty other files for the sake of space.

```
226 Transfer complete.
```

```
FTP> i
200 Type set to I.
```

The **i** command sets the transfer mode as binary, which is necessary to preserve the program's integrity.

```
FTP> get disinfectant-36.hqx
220 PORT command successful.
150 Opening ASCII mode data connection for disinfectant-36.hqx
226 (214490 bytes). Transfer complete.
217810 bytes received in 422.3 seconds (0.5037 Kbytes/s)
local: disinfectant-36.hqx remote: disinfectant-36.hqx
```

```
FTP>quit
```

Variations

One complicating factor in the process can be local file naming conventions. UNIX allows long filenames, but some systems have narrow limitations. VM/CMS, for instance, requires file-names in two words, neither of which can be longer than eight characters. So, CMS users will have to create new filenames to match their system since UNIX filenames do not match the CMS naming convention.

In previous examples, you simply saw the **get** command fol-lowed by the filename exactly as it appears in the FTP server's di-rectory listing. Here, in order to rename the file so that it will be accepted on the CMS operating system, the new filename is added to the command string. The protocol is **get filename new-file.name.** A period in the new filename will show up as a space on the CMS system, thus putting the filename into two words. Here's how the command looks:

FTP>get disinfectant-36.hqx disinfec.hqx

The file will appear in a CMS user's file list as DISINFEC HQX. Note that the user wisely chose to keep the BinHex extension (.hqx) as part of the new filename. That will help remind him or her that the file is software and must be downloaded in binary format.

9

Graphic Browsers

9.1 Introduction

Graphic browsers are credited with spurring much of the World Wide Web's recent rise in popularity. Soon after the release of Mosaic, developed by the National Center for Supercomputer Applications at the University of Illinois, use of the Web began a dramatic rise that continues today. And in a circular relationship, the rapid growth of the Web inspires more graphic browsers. The Web's growth will probably level off at some point, but for the immediate future, graphic access to the Web is going to be an exciting ride.

Graphic browsers differ from the original text-only browsers in that they not only have a graphic interface — users of Macintosh and Microsoft Windows operating systems are familiar with graphic interfaces, with their windows, icons, buttons, and menus — but can also display graphic images, including photographs, animations, and video. Most graphic browsers today don't actually play sound and display video, but they facilitate the process by opening "helper applications." For instance, if you select a link to a video clip, your web browser will look in your computer's directories for a program that can display video. Many Macintosh users have a program called Sparkle, which browsers will recognize and launch when they encounter video clips. Sparkle then shows the clip the browser has downloaded.

The situation is changing fast, though, and by the time this book is released, browsers will likely be much more sophisticated than they are now. Java, a new programming language recently released by Sun Microsystems, is even now redefining what the

Web is and does. Browsers are incorporating Java capability by using HotJava, a Java interpreter. Java will allow small application programs, called "applets," to be downloaded with documents, providing whatever functions — animation, video, audio — are required by the writers of the document. That means the days of helper applications like Sparkle may be numbered. Necessary applications will be delivered over the Net rather than residing on users' machines. That new capability is expected to change the Web dramatically. See http://www.javasoft.com/index.html for more information.

In this chapter, we will cover some basic information about graphic browsers. Netscape is the most popular and arguably the best of the freely available browsers. Mosaic, still available but no longer being developed and updated, was the first graphic browser to capture the attention of the Internet community. Microsoft's Internet Explorer has quickly become Netscape's chief competitor. We do not include a specific section on it only because we have little experience using it. However, its range of features and sophistication are comparable to Netscape's. See http://www.microsoft.com/ie/default.asp for more information.

9.2 Netscape

Introduction

Netscape provides fast and sophisticated access to the Web. Current reports indicate that it holds about 60 to 70 percent of the browser market. Whether this number is accurate or not, few people dispute that it is the most popular web browser. Netscape Communications Corporation, creator of the Netscape browser, develops secure World Wide Web browsers for business and government. The company also provides browsers at no charge for educational use (see Figure 9.1).

Netscape tends to be assertive about developing features that include new HyperText Markup Language (HTML) functions. (HTML is the coding used to create web pages.) As a result, Netscape generates a certain amount of controversy in the web community because the enhancements often are not yet accepted parts of the current standard, which means they will not work if the same page is viewed through another browser. As a particularly notorious example, Netscape introduced a feature that lets web page designers make particular words or phrases blink. No other browser supports the <blink></blink> tag (the term *tag* refers to in-

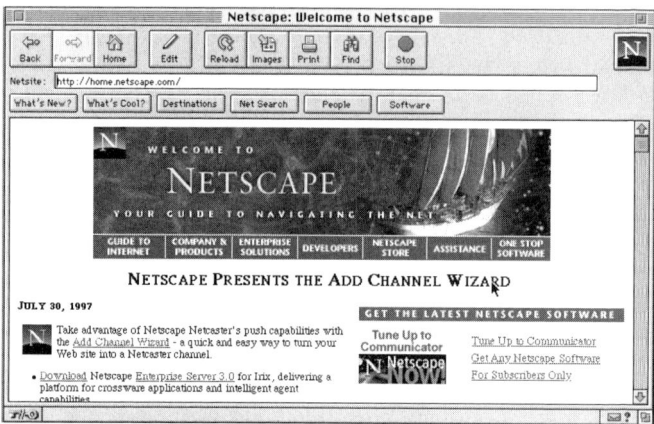

Figure 9.1   Copyright 1996 Netscape Communications Corp. Used with permission. All rights reserved. This page may not be reprinted or copied without the express written permission of Netscape.

structions the browser follows when presenting a document; they are invisible to viewers of the document), so if someone looks at a page with blinking text in it via MacWeb, for instance, the words will appear as they do normally, not as blinking.

Netscape continues to grow in popularity in part because its enhancements give more control over page appearance to HTML authors, allowing them to change font size, add color, animate images, and so on. One of the added features in Netscape 2.0 is something called "frames." These allow web page authors to create separate windows within the browser's main window. The author can then design pages so that new documents can appear within those inner windows. It is a feature that has web developers very excited. Netscape also tends to be faster than most other graphic browsers because it can open up more than one connection to a server at once. That means it can download text and graphic files at the same time, putting pieces of a page together simultaneously rather than sequentially. Other browsers may load text first, then each image file in turn.

Netscape Navigator 3.0 for the Macintosh takes up a little more than 3MB of hard disk space for the application itself and requires about 9MB of RAM to run.

Netscape built-in features

Graphic browsers generally include built-in features to help you get around the sometimes confusing world of the Web. Two of the most helpful are the Bookmark (or Hotlist) feature and the History feature, both of which help you keep track of where you've been.

Bookmark

Netscape's Bookmark feature is a menu listing sites you've visited that you may wish to visit again. It is a user-extendible list of web sites. When you find an interesting page, go to the Bookmarks menu and choose Add Bookmark. Netscape also allows you to re-arrange bookmarks and organize them under different headers by using the Bookmarks option under the Window menu.

History

Netscape's History feature is found under the Window menu. It keeps track of all the places you visit during your current session. If you decide you want to return to a site you visited previously, you can choose it from the Go menu rather than using the Back button to retrace your steps one page at a time. Netscape also has directory buttons and a Directory menu that contain links to various resources provided by the company, including links to its pages. This feature can be handy for finding out more information about the browser itself and its capabilities.

Show Location

This option, found under the Options menu, is convenient to have available. If you activate the Show Location option, you get a narrow box near the top of the window that shows the URL of your current location. This feature will help you get the correct URL for when you need to cite for a research paper. Into that box you can also type or paste URLs that you want to visit.

Default page

Graphic browsers give users the freedom to choose any starting location, meaning the web page that automatically appears every time you start the program. This is known as the default page. Netscape comes with its starting point set at Netscape Communications' homepage. One problem with leaving this as the default page is that Netscape's servers are sometimes busy, so when you start you may get an error message saying the server you chose is not available. It's generally a good idea to change the default to a web page you are likely to use regularly. Ideally, you should set a web page on your computer so that the starting place is always available. One possibility is to set a simple page that contains a list of frequently visited URLs, a kind of page-based hotlist or bookmarks list.

To change the default location, first go to the page you want to have as your starting location. If the page is located at a remote location, choose Open Location from the File menu. If the page is located on your own computer, choose Open File from the File menu. Select the URL in the location box, copy it, then go to the Options menu and select General Preferences. In General Preferences, there is a category, which usually appears by default, called Startup. In that dialog box there is a box for the Home Page Location. Paste in the URL you copied. Close General Preferences by selecting the OK button.

Other interface elements

When you start using any browser, it's probably a good idea to keep all its elements in view so that you know at a glance what your options and possibilities are. However, as you become more familiar with Netscape's interface, you may wish to display more window space. Netscape also lets you toggle the toolbar, locations, and directory buttons, making them visible or hidden whenever you wish. For example, if your connection to the Net is slow or unstable, you may want to turn off Auto Load Images under the Options menu. Images take much longer to download than text, even under good conditions. If connection conditions are poor, image loading can make browsing the Web a slow, frustrating experience.

E-mail

One very convenient feature of sophisticated graphic browsers like Netscape is their ability to serve as communication as well as information tools. You can send e-mail from within Netscape as long as the preferences file includes your mail server and e-mail address. If you select a link on a web page created by the <mailto:user@host>tag (commonly used by web page maintainers as a convenient way for readers to provide feedback about the contents of their pages), Netscape will automatically give you the mail feature. E-mail can be used at any time, however, whether a mail to link is available or not. It is often used to e-mail the contents of a page to someone who does not have access to the Web or to send a URL to someone who you think might be interested in a site you've discovered. To do so, choose Mail Document from the File menu.

To enter your server and e-mail address, select Mail and News Preferences from the Options menu. Then select the Identity tag. There, you will find four boxes to fill out: Your Name, Your Email, Reply-to-Address, and Your Organization. Fill out the boxes completely. The mail server entry is likely to be whatever is to the right of the @ symbol in your e-mail address (that's not always the case, so it might be a good idea to check with local computing service people to verify the correct setting). In Eric's case, he would type **showme.missouri.edu** in the Mail server box and **wleric@showme.missouri.edu** in the E-mail box.

Netscape 3.0 can also be used as an off-line e-mail reader. If your system includes a POP server (if you're not sure, ask your computing support people), you can use Netscape to download e-mail to your computer, where you can read it — and reply if you like — at your leisure without having to remain connected to the system. To do so, you need to add some information to Netscape's preferences. Go to the Options menu and choose Mail and News Preferences. Choose the Servers tab and fill in the boxes for Outgoing Mail (SMTP) Server, Incoming Mail (POP) Server, and POP User ID. It may be worth consulting local computing services people to make sure you get the addresses correct. If you have limited hard disk space you may wish to limit the maximum size of incoming mail. The option for doing so is right below the POP User ID box. The next option lets you choose to move your mail to your computer or download copies, leaving the originals on the server. The latter is useful if you are reading mail on a machine other than the one on which you want to store any important mail. If you leave mail on the server, the same batch of mail (plus any new e-mail) will arrive the next time you use Netscape to download your mail. The last e-mail option lets you ask Netscape to fetch your mail at specific intervals. If you leave the default setting, Never, selected, you need to tell Netscape each time you want it to download your mail.

After you have made all the changes to the mail preferences that you want to, click on the OK button to close the preferences dialog box, then go to the Window menu and select Netscape Mail. Netscape will ask you to supply your system password. After you do, it will transfer your mail and present you with three frames, one to show your mailboxes, one to show the contents of the selected mailbox, and one to show the contents of individual notes.

Netnews

Netscape serves as a fairly sophisticated news reader. If you wish to read Usenet newsgroups, or Netnews, via Netscape, the browser offers many of the features found on programs designed specifically as news readers. To use the Netnews feature, go to the Mail and News Preferences, and enter the address of a Netnews server. If you aren't sure of the Netnews server address at your school, check with your computer support center.

View Source

One of the best ways to learn how to create your own web pages is to study the pages already on the Web. Many graphic browsers have a feature called View Source, which launches a text editor to display the HTML used to create the page you see with the browser. This feature lets you compare what a page looks like with its underlying structure in HTML. The HTML source of any page you are viewing can be displayed either by Netscape or in any word processor or text editor of your choice. Under the Options menu, choose General Preferences, then click on the Applications tab. Beside the View Source option, you can check the Netscape box or click on the Browse button and then select the program of your choice. If you choose a program other than Netscape, whenever you choose the Document Source under the View menu, that program will be automatically launched and a new file created with the contents of the web page you are viewing. Netscape 3.0 also includes, under the View menu, a Document Info option, which offers information about the document, not including its HTML contents. It tells the document's location, lists URLs for images, gives modification dates, etc. Netscape 3.0 also includes Frame Source and Frame Info options. To view the source or get information about a document in a specific frame, first click once in the frame to select it, then go to the View menu and choose the option you want.

It's common practice to borrow structural and design elements from web pages. HTML seen under the View Source feature is sometimes used as a template for creating new pages. Be careful, though, not to reproduce web page content without permission. For example, if you come across an essay that includes animated graphics of plant growth, you could borrow the HTML method for producing animated graphics, but you shouldn't use the images of plants used on that page unless you get permission from the person who created them or holds any copyrights to them.

Where to find Netscape Navigator copies and information

Homepage
http://home.Netscape.com/

Download page
http://home.Netscape.com/comprod/mirror/index.html

Software FTP sites
wuarchive.wustl.edu/packages/www/Netscape/netscape1.1/
ftp.cps.cmich.edu/pub/Netscape/
ftp.utdallas.edu/pub/Netscape/netscape1.1/
ftp.micro.caltech.edu/pub/Netscape/
unicron.unomaha.edu/pub/Netscape/netscape 1.1/
server.berkeley.edu/pub/Netscape/
SunSITE.unc.edu/pub/packages/infosystems/WWW/clients/
   Netscape/
magic.umeche.maine.edu/pub/Mirrors/nscape/consult.ocis.
temple.edu/Big_Kahuna/Pub/Mac/Comm/ (Mac only)

9.3 Mosaic

Introduction

For more than a year, Mosaic ruled the Web (see Figure 9.2). Appearing early in 1993, Mosaic was the first graphic browser to be widely adopted around the Net. It has been credited not only with capturing the imaginations of Net users from traditional domains (education, government, and military) but also with attracting the attention of the business community. In fact, it appeared for a while that Mosaic might follow such brand names as Kleenex and Xerox by becoming both a name for a specific product and a generic term. People were beginning to refer to "Mosaic" as both the browser and the Web itself.

Marc Andreeson lead the team that created Mosaic at the National Center for Supercomputing Applications (NCSA). In March 1994, Andreeson, along with several of his colleagues, left the center and began developing a commercial version of the browser, called Netscape, which quickly surpassed Mosaic as the most popular web browser.

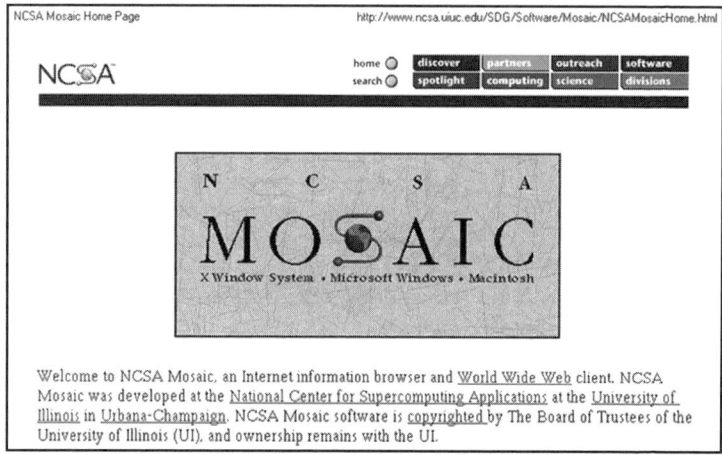

Figure 9.2

Still, Mosaic had a powerful effect on many people, especially on those who had previously been skeptical about the Web's range of possibilities. Stories of conversions from skeptic to believer are common. Users' eyes would pop when they saw how the combination of voice, text, image, and color and the easy point-and-click graphic interface enhanced the hypertextual organization of the Web.

Mosaic for Macintosh version 2.01 requires about 5MB of RAM and takes up about 2MB of hard disk space. NCSA announced in January 1997 that it considered the development of Mosaic to be complete, so although copies will remain available, support will be reduced, and new versions will not be forthcoming.

Homepage

Here are the URLs for different versions of the Mosaic homepage. Each is slightly different and offers information specific to the Mosaic browser designed for each operating system listed.

All-purpose Mosaic homepage
http://www.ncsa.uiuc.edu/SDG/Software/Mosaic/
NCSAMosaicHome.html

MacMosaic homepage
http://www.ncsa.uiuc.edu/SDG/Software/MacMosaic/
MacMosaicHome.html

WindowsMosaic homepage
http://www.ncsa.uiuc.edu/SDG/Software/WinMosaic/
HomePage.html

XWindowsMosaic homepage
http://www.ncsa.uiuc.edu/SDG/Software/XMosaic/

9.4 The Future of the Web

As we're finishing revisions to *Writing Online,* the "browser wars" continue to escalate. Netscape and Microsoft are the main players in this game, and each has ambitious and sophisticated new products slated for release before this book comes off the presses. It is impossible to predict exactly what the web terrain and its tools will look like six months from now, but we can offer a few educated guesses.

For one thing, the browser seems about to be engulfed by a bigger, more flexible suite of tools packaged together. It will become only one option from among a number of web tools. Netscape and Microsoft's Internet Explorer have already begun the process by including e-mail functions and netnews readers in their browsers, but the next generation of programs will top that by including conferencing, chat, and calendar programs as well. Netscape's new product, Communicator, is an example of the new genre of web tool.

Another new twist that has the potential to radically affect the Web and how it's used is "push" technology. Both Netscape and Microsoft are promoting new features in their products that will allow information providers the capability of serving content in a timely way by "pushing" it to clients' browsers. Push technologies have gotten a good deal of attention, some of it enthusiastic, some of it concerned. They bring to the Web broadcasting functions similar to what television has provided, and that means both convenience and some loss of control for information consumers.

Whether bigger and better browsers and push technologies give you thrills or chills, they at least suggest that the Web will continue to grow and become an ever-richer source of information and communication for the foreseeable future.

9.5 A Selection of URLs to Explore

http://WWW.w3.org/hypertext/WWW/History.html
A timeline of the World Wide Web's development
http://WWW.w3.org/

Homepage for W3, the World Wide Web Consortium, a collection of people and organizations working to continue the development of the Web
http://www.yahoo.com/Computers/Internet/World_Wide_Web/
Yahoo's World Wide Web directory

10

MOOs and MUDs

10.1 Introduction

MOOs and MUDs are Internet software that allow users to meet online to converse, play games, hold classes and academic conferences, or — if a person registers as a member of a particular MOO or MUD — create a virtual room of one's own. MUD stands for multiuser dimension (or dungeon since MUDs are often used for playing Dungeons and Dragons). MOO stands for MUD — object-oriented. Object-oriented refers to a kind of programming language that lets programmers share bits of programs they write so that others can incorporate those bits into their own programs.

Because MOOs and MUDs are still associated with game playing and diversion, rather than work and academics, many schools do not allow students to access them during peak operating hours. Some ban them outright. However, more and more academic work is being done in MOOs and MUDs. They are being used for distance education classes, for cross-class collaboration, academic conferencing, and for learning foreign languages, to name only a few examples. Since most of our work occurs in MOOs, the following examples and explanations will be from MOOs. However, most of the commands can be used in MUDs as well. In a MUD or MOO, whenever you are uncertain or confused, type **help** and hit the Enter key.

10.2 Telnet Help for MOOing

Since many schools do not offer support for using MOOs, most users' first experiences in MOOing are via telnet.

73

Telnet, you may recall from Chapter 6, is an Internet tool that allows a person to connect to a remote computer. It allows the person's terminal to activate commands on the remote computer even though it may be on the other side of the world. Although that sounds exotic, it's really quite simple in concept. Connecting via telnet is like making a phone call, only instead of dialing a number, you input an address.

To telnet, you need to know the address you want to reach. Often you'll see addresses for MOOs given in "telnet." Someone might write, "To get to SomeMOO, telnet moo.somemoo.com 7777," which means to reach SomeMOO, you would type the following at your Internet account prompt:

prompt%telnet moo.somemoo.com 7777

It is important not to put a space before typing the word *telnet*. Make sure you *do* put a space between *telnet* and the address, and a space between the final portion of the address name (in this case, .com) and the port number (in this case, 7777).

Viewing a MOO in telnet

Telnet, though it will connect you to a MOO, is not a MOO client, such as TinyFugue or MUDDweller. It is a generic Internet tool designed for connecting to a remote computer. Therefore, when you telnet to a MOO, there is no separate window or line for writing a message, then sending it; there is no automatic word wrap on the right margin, and the text does not automatically stop scrolling by before you can read it. Telnet merely accesses the software. A MOO or MUD client manages the MOO/MUD so that you can control margins, scroll, and send messages with greater ease.

MOOs do have commands that let you correct for the scrolling and word wrap problems you'll get with a telnet connection; however, they cannot provide a separate window for writing your message. The scroll and wrap commands are **@pagelength** and **@linelength**, respectively.

To use these, do the following:

1. Telnet to a MOO.
2. Connect to the MOO. The command for this will be **co guest.**
3. Once in the MOO, type (as an example) **@pagelength 22.**
4. Then type (as an example) **@linelength 75.**

(You can experiment with different numbers to see what reads best in your screen.) In some MOOs, this command automatically activates word wrap so that words don't break at odd places on the right margin. In other MOOs, you need to type the command for word wrapping. You'll know if you need it because the MOO will send you a message that says, "linelength now 75, word wrapping is off." Some MOOs lose their word wrapping when the line length is changed. If the MOO doesn't send you a message, but still loses automatic word wrap when the line length is changed, you'll be able to tell because some of the words at the right margin will break in the middle and carry over to the next line. The command to activate word wrapping is **@wrap on**.

Once you have set the line length and made sure the word wrap feature of the MOO is active, the right margin will take care of itself. However, to manage scrolling, you will need to signal the MOO when you're ready to read the next screen of messages. When you use **@pagelength**, the MOO will stop text from scrolling after the designated number of lines have scrolled onto the screen. You will see a line at the end of the text that says:

****More***** (# of lines) @more:rest:flush to continue.

If you type **@more**, you will get the next twenty-two lines of text. You will keep getting screens of text in twenty-two-line increments every time you type **@more**.

If you type **@rest**, the text that is waiting will scroll by without stopping, even if it is more than the twenty-two lines you set as your page length.

If you type **@flush**, the text that is in the queue waiting to be read by you will be erased, and you'll see the first new message in the discussion since you typed **@flush**.

The **@more** command comes in especially handy if you decide to read a MOO's newspaper or some of its help files. You will also find it useful when you are in a fast-moving discussion. As you take time to write a message — and in telnet interfaces, messaging takes time because it is hard to see what you are writing — messages from others who are in the room talking with you will be backed up for you, allowing you to speak and hear (write and read) at your leisure.

Sending a message in telnet

This is an unwieldy task. In telnet interfaces on MOOs, you don't have a separate place for writing a message; instead, you must write on the same screen — in the same space — from which the messages you are reading emerge. Thus as you are entering a message, incoming messages interrupt your flow of writing.

In a MOO, to send a message, you type the command **say** (or its shortcut ") and then the text of your message. So if you were to say hello to someone in the room, you might type "**hi there, how are you?** After you press the Enter key, the message will be sent. You would then see on your screen:

> You say, "hi there, how are you?"

Here's how writing a message looks in telnet when, as you are writing, others are speaking.

> "I really wish there Zeus says, "The god's must be crazy" was a way to
> Athena [to Zeus] "well yes, if they start by hiding in the mother and
>   to write these castrating
> their father." ages without so much hecticness.

On a split screen, with a separate window for writing, the same words would look like this:

> Zeus says, "The god's must be crazy"
> Athena [to Zeus]: well yes, if they start by hiding in the mother and
>   castrating their father.

> "I really wish there was a way to write these messages without so
>   much hecticness.

This feature, more than any other, compels MOO regulars to find a client.

10.3 Alternatives to Telnet

Clients, programs designed for specific uses, such as e-mail, or in this case working in a MOO, are the best alternatives to telnet. Which client you use depends on how you are connected to the Internet. The best place to go to learn all you need to know about clients is Jennifer Smith's FREQUENTLY ASKED QUESTIONS: MUD Clients and Servers at http://www.cs.okstate.edu/~jds/

mudfaq-p2.htm. There you'll find a complete client resource. Here we list clients we have used or have had recommended to us. Remember to download all files associated with the client of your choice. Usually these include the word *README* in their name.

UNIX

TinyFugue

Nick prefers this UNIX client. TinyFugue allows users to automate for frequently used MOO/MUD commands and greetings. It can also be set to log into your most frequently used MOO or MUD automatically. TinyFugue can be found at:

FTP to: ftp.tcp.com Path: /pub/mud/Clients
FTP to: muds.okstate.edu Path: /pub/jds/clients/UnixClients

VMS

tfVMS

This is not something either of us has used, but since Nick likes TinyFugue so much, we thought we'd mention its VMS version. This is available at:

FTP to: muds.okstate.edu Path: /pub/jds/clients/VMSClients

PC

WinWorld

This is used with Microsoft Windows with a Winsock connection. It is available at:

FTP to: ftp.mgl.ca Path: /pub/winworld
FTP to: papa.indstate.edu Path: /winsock-l/mud

Pueblo

This is used with Windows95 and Windows/NT with a Winsock connection. This is a very powerful client that allows for interactive hypertext as well as MOOing. As more MUDs and MOOs move to web interfaces, the value of this client will grow. It is available at:

http://www.chaco.com/pueblo/

Macintosh

MUDDweller

This is a nice little tool. It has its own communications software so that you can use it via a standard modem connection, or you can use it with MacTCP. It is available at:

FTP to: rudolf.ethz.ch Path: /pub/mud
FTP to: mac.archive.umich.edu Path: /mac/util/comm
FTP to: ftp.tcp.com Path: /pub/mud/Clients

MacMOOSE

If you do have a MacTCP connection, get this client. It will give you more flexibility. It is available at:

FTP to: ftp.media.mit.edu Path: /pub/asb/MacMOOSE/
http://asb.www.media.mit.edu/people/asb/MacMOOSE/

11

A MOO Walkthrough (Telnet)

CHAPTER CONTENTS

11.1 Introduction

11.2 MOO Etiquette

11.1 Introduction

This is a sample session we put together from a composite of rooms we have at different MOOs. SomeMOO is an imaginary MOO with real rooms in it. We purposefully compiled this as a way to give you a sense of how you might move about a MOO and use certain help commands. In this section, we activate the help commands so that you can see here what you will see on your screen. We suggest that the best way to use this chapter is to have it open when you log into a MOO or MUD for the first time. In this section, you will also meet Munchkin, the standard MOO example character. Munchkin first appears when we show you the help say command.

To begin the walkthrough, we telnet to our imaginary MOO.

prompt% **telnet moo.somemoo.com 7777**
Trying...
Connected to moo.somemoo.com.
Escape character is '^]'.

Once connected, the following menu typically greets the user:

Type:
COnnect [Name] [password]   connect as existing player
CReate [Name] [password]   create a temporary player (not all
    MOOs have this)

COnnect Guest   connect as a guest

@who or Who	see who's here now
@quit or Quit	quit SomeMOO

With a telnet interface, there is no prompt. The commands are typed in the flush-left, bottom portion of the screen.

@who
No one logged in.
co guest
*** Created ***
Welcome Station
You are inside a MOO Highway rest stop. You can grab a map, grab a snack, read the newspaper, The SomeMOO Times, or exit through the door to the north.
Obvious exits: north to the SomeMOO bus stop (catch a ride to town), south to virtual rest rooms, east to maps and vending machines, west to the newstand.
You see a note, a friendly tour guide, and a lost mitten.

We will move through three rooms. The Electric Pen and The Writery are rooms Nick and Eric have built in DaedalusMOO, a MOO sponsored and maintained by The Daedalus Group, designers of networked writing software used in many classrooms. For teachers who use Daedalus software in their classrooms, this MOO is a place to bring students for online conferencing and class meetings or to arrange collaborative projects across classes. The third room, The TechnoRhetoricians Bar and Grill, belongs to Eric. Its home is at MediaMOO, a MOO used by media researchers. MediaMOO is not a MOO for classes or student meetings.

@join nickc
The Electric Pen
It's a bit cluttered, of course, and you can't help noticing the sprawled sheaf of papers on the floor that break the occasional fall of a floppy disk from the teetering stack on the table above. Next to that table, in front of the window, an espresso machine sits on top of a dorm-style refrigerator. Around the room, along the walls, sit a set of matching chairs, a couch, and end-tables, with a coffee table in the center marred by cat scratches on the legs. The window is open slightly, letting a cool breeze waft in. Obvious exits: tw to The Writery.

You see Bookcase here.
nickc is here.

Whenever you first enter a room, you are given its description. In this example, nickc built himself a grander office than he had at the time as a teaching assistant, where he met students in a basement office cramped with steam pipes and broken file cabinets. The description might also include other players who are in the room. You can talk to any player who is in the same room as you. Since MOOs are multiuser, there can be, depending on the circumstances, quite a few users.

@pagelength 24
Page length is now 24.
@linelength 80
Line length is now 80. Word wrapping is off.
@wrap on
Word wrap is now on.

Remember the importance of these commands for telnetters.

The **help communication** command is an example of using the help menu. Under this command, you will see a number of other commands for communicating with fellow MOOers:

say (or ")	Talk to the other players in the room
whisper	Talk privately to someone in the same room
emote	Nonverbal communication with others in the same room
page	Shout to a person in another or the same room
gagging	Screen out noise generated by certain other players
news	Read the wizards' most recent set of general announcements
@gripe	End complaints to the wizards
@typo @bug @idea @suggest	
	Send complaints or ideas to the owner of the current room
whereis	Locate other players
@who	Find out who is currently logged in
mail	The MOO e-mail system
security	The facilities for detecting forged messages and eavesdropping

Each of these commands leads to more specific help. Some examples follow.

If you type **help say**, you'll see the following:

Says anything out loud so that everyone in the same room hears it. This is so commonly used that there's a special abbreviation for it, the double quote (").

Munchkin types this:	"This is a great MOO!
Munchkin sees this:	You say, "This is a great MOO!"
Others in the same room see this:	Munchkin says, "This is a great MOO!"

The help files for MOOs are pretty much the same from MOO to MOO for basic commands. MOO software is available on the Net and can be set up on any Internet server. After that, each MOO wizard, the person in charge of maintaining the MOO, will make his or her own customizations, often with the help of other wizards and members of the MOO community. MOOs evolve over time.

We'll also show you the syntax and official MOO examples for emote and page since they are frequently used.

If you type **help emote,** you'll see the following:

Announces anything to everyone in the same room. This is commonly used to express various nonverbal forms of communication. The abbreviation for the emote command is the colon (:)

Munchkin types this:	:wishes he were much taller...
Everyone in the same room sees this:	Munchkin wishes he were much much taller...

If you type **help page**, you'll see the following:

Sends a message to a connected player, telling them your location and, optionally, text.

Type page [player] [text].

Munchkin types this:	Page Frebble with "Where are you?"
Frebble sees this:	You sense that Munchkin is looking for you in the Kitchen.
Then Frebble sees this:	"Where are you?"
Munchkin sees this:	Your message has been received.

The **look** command helps you get your bearings. It's helpful if you forget where exits are or who is in the room with you.

> look
> The Electric Pen
> Long room description deleted here for brevity.
> Obvious exits: tw to The Writery
> You see Bookcase here.
> nickc is here.

To move from room to room, follow the exits by typing the command given after the obvious exits listed. Simply typing **tw** will move you to another room called The Writery. This is the meeting room for the Online Writery in DaedalusMOO. Students at the University of Missouri can login and come here to meet a writing tutor online to discuss their writing.

> tw
> The Writery
> More of an aroma than a room. You're reminded of baking bread. Rich coffee brewing. Warmth. Safety. Comfort. Donut holes. Community. Fingers stuck together with glaze. But there's something else cooking here. Not bread, but . . . (type: read welcome) [Note: conversations here may be logged, but only for record-keeping purposes.]
> Obvious exits: east to TR Bar and Grill, tep to The Electric Pen
> Eric (idling away -- back soon) and Nick (drowsing . . . feel free to wake) are here.

We'll travel again, this time to a bar. The actual location of TechnoRhetoricians' Bar and Grill is the MediaMOO.

> east
> The TechnoRhetoricians' Bar and Grill
> A slovenly, comfortable hovel where the patrons discuss the rhetorical implications of every little thing, including the shifting dunes of crumbs and peanut shells that ripple across the floor. No one here is daunted by triviality.
> Obvious exits: north to the panopticon, west to The Writery, east to MOOReligion Courtyard, down to The Cell, and up to CWTA Outpost

You see MacXVI, Lou the Bartender, Pony, Isocrates, Derrida, tool box, and Barthes here. MC, sm, Glenn, Eric [GPC], and beckster are here.

These represent the basic commands. The final command you need to know is how to leave a MOO, which is @quit.

@quit
Connection closed by foreign host.

11.2   MOO Etiquette

1. The first time you visit any MOO, you will login as a guest. Almost every MOO will have a welcome message for guests. In the message, there will often be directions for how to read the MOO's policies and guidelines for behavior. For example, the welcome message might advise you to read the acceptable use policy by typing **read aup**. If for some reason the MOO does not give you a direction like this, the following suggestions should keep you a guest in good standing.

2. Many MOOs are educational sites. Classes may be meeting. Students from across the country may be collaborating on projects. Don't interrupt this work by barging into a room and asking if anyone wants to talk.

3. When you log into a MOO, the first room you land in is usually a common room. Very often the rooms immediately off it have useful information and are considered public spaces. If you see another player in one of these rooms, the polite thing to do is say hello.

4. As you explore a MOO, you will move from room to room. The process will feel as if you are wandering in a labyrinth. However, many MOOs have maps as navigational aids. The help map command will tell you if the MOO you are in has a map and how to use it.

5. If you plan to visit a particular MOO regularly, you should request a character. **Help character** or **help register** commands will tell you whom to send e-mail to in order to do that. Many MOOs include this information in their welcome message or acceptable use file.

6. Sometimes as you are exploring a MOO and using the navigational commands to move from room to room, you will inadvertently enter a room while the owner and, perhaps, another player are in it. If so, they will usually say hello. Say hello back, and let them know that you are just exploring. They may or may not wish to talk at that time. They might be building an object or doing some work. Therefore, if you wish to talk, always ask first if now is a good time for them to chat. Never launch into a conversation in these circumstances.

7. When you are done exploring a MOO, always use the @quit command to leave. This helps the MOO run more efficiently.

12

OWLs and Other Birds of the Net

12.1 OWLs

OWLs are not virtual birds of prey swooping around the Internet looking for hapless technorodents. They are writing center services that have migrated to the Net. OWL is an acronym for Online Writing Lab and more than a few of them have sprung up in the past several years. They are sources of information and assistance for student writers.

With a few exceptions (such as Dakota State's OWL), online writing labs are being developed by people who run face-to-face writing centers. Unlike their place–bound predecessors, though, OWLs generally are available as resources for students from anywhere on the Internet, another case where the Net is crossing traditional boundaries. They will not, nor are they generally intended to, replace traditional writing centers. But online writing services and resources do offer things that are not available (at least not as conveniently) from traditional writing centers.

OWLs come in all shapes and sizes. Some consist mainly of an e-mail address where tutors respond to inquiries or read and comment on drafts of papers. Others are elaborate combinations of web pages, e-mail access, mailing lists, newsgroups, and MOOs. What all seem to have in common is providing student writers with assistance they cannot find in most classes.

Some OWLs provide writing reference material on mechanics and grammar; organization and idea generation; online versions of common writers' aids like dictionaries, thesauri, and style guides; sample papers; and sometimes essays by tutors offering writing advice. Some OWLs provide access to tutors via e-mail or MOOs so that students can ask questions about writing or submit drafts of papers for review.

The information or assistance that remote students can expect from an OWL may vary dramatically from one service to another. Keep in mind that even though they exist on the Internet, these services are sometimes limited by local conditions. Most OWLs must give priority to serving students at their own institutions. Some, however, welcome people from anywhere. For example, Purdue University's OWL (one of the first and most popular) currently focuses on offering information about writing based on the printed handouts developed by its writing lab. Once the information has been provided for Purdue students, the university incurs very little additional expense in making it available to anyone on the Internet. Many people from places around the world have taken advantage of that resource.

The University of Missouri's Online Writery (http://www.missouri.edu/~writery) offers "cybertutors," people who are paid to help whoever inquires. Although priority is given to the university's students, cybertutors often end up talking to as many nonuniversity people (some of whom are not even students) as they do local students. This is the main distinction between OWLs and most traditional writing centers, where limitations on who can use the service are usually enforced strictly.

12.2   WIOLEs

WIOLE, or Writing Intensive Online Learning Environment, is a cousin to the OWL and has many similar characteristics, including network access to writing tutors and information about writing. The fundamental purpose of WIOLEs is to facilitate written conversation online. Conversations may include helping students with papers, but the emphasis is more on electronic written conversation as a legitimate end itself rather than merely as a means of improving printed texts. The emphasis might be said to shift from developing texts to developing ideas. Both OWLs, which are prevalent and growing in number, and WIOLEs, which emerge as key elements in online writing education, are valuable resources for students exploring the Net. The University of Missouri's Online Writery is an example of a WIOLE (see Figure 12.1). In addition to its OWL services and web pages, it includes two

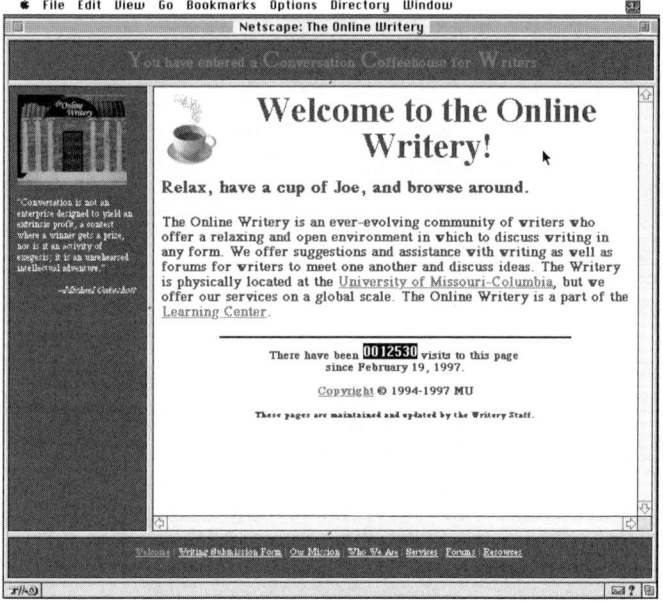

Figure 12.1

mailing lists, two local newsgroups, and a MOO, giving students several channels through which to converse—synchronously or asynchronously. Certainly, Internet Relay Chat (IRC) could also serve as a venue for synchronous, or real-time, conversation.

12.3 List of Sites

The URLs listed here point to OWLs and WIOLEs that you might want to visit. We recommend that you explore a number of them to find the ones that might best fit your needs and interests. Of course, this list is by no means comprehensive. But because most of these sites include links to other similar services, visiting one generally gives access to all. It's a matter of following the links until you find what you need.

We have not listed OWLs that primarily consist of e-mail. Some of those services may not be prepared for large numbers of inquiries, whereas others invite anyone to seek help from them. The Purdue OWL web pages, however, include a page with OWL e-mail addresses. We recommend looking there for a current list.

The parenthetical notes indicate our impression of the site's current main focus. Some sites have plans to expand their services, but have not yet developed those new services. "Local information" indicates that the site mainly provides information online about the local face-to-face writing center. "Writing information" means the site provides access to writing guides and help files. "Conversation" means the site provides access to tutors who are available to discuss writing over the Net.

National Writing Centers Association List of Online Writing Labs and Centers
http://www2.colgate.edu/diw/NWCAOWLS.html
(comprehensive and annotated lists of OWLs)

Bowling Green University
Gopher://Gopher.bgsu.edu:70/11/Departments/write (writing information)

The CyberspaceWriting Center Consultation Project (WritingWorks)
http://fur.rscc.cc.tn.us/cyberproject.html
(conversation)

Dakota State University
http://www.dsu.edu/departments/liberal/cola/OWL/
(conversation)

Purdue University
http://owl.english.purdue.edu/
(writing information)

Rensselaer Polytechnic Institute
http://www.rpi.edu/dept/llc/writecenter/web/home.html
(writing information)

Trinity College
http://www.trincoll.edu/writcent/aksmith.html
(writing information, conversation)

The University of Michigan-Ann Arbor
http://www.lsq.umich.edu/ecb/OWL/owl.html
(writing information, conversation)

The University of Missouri-Columbia
http://www.missouri.edu/~writery
(conversation)

13

How to Create Your Own Basic Web Page

13.1 The Web Changes Everything

The Web opens up new possibilities that just do not exist in a print-dominated world. Much of the hype surrounds the multimedia capability of the Web, the ease with which it allows writers to employ sound and image along with words. That's important, of course, but print already allows the juxtaposition of word and image, and sound recording is an accessible technology. What the Web does that is so radical is put control of those various media into the hands of anyone with access and allows them to create with the media in new ways. Word, sound, and image can interact on the Web in ways they cannot with other technologies.

The publishing playing field is dramatically leveled, and the tools available to students and other writers are nearly as sophisticated as those available to large organizations and companies. The Web does not, by itself, democratize publishing, but it creates the conditions in which democratization is more likely to occur. Much of the information on the Web now, even on some of the "coolest" web pages, was put there not by professional writers and designers and scholars, but by whoever wanted to put it there. English students may view the Web not only as a place to find information but also as a place to put information. By adding their own work and ideas to the growing body of knowledge on the Net, writing starts to have a whole new meaning.

Creating web pages is not difficult. The learning curve for hypertext markup language is steep for about five minutes, then things level out and you're on your way. In fact, the learning curve is lessening. There are many programs available on the Net called HTML editors — many of them freeware or shareware — and some of them are getting very sophisticated. The need to learn HTML tags, or the commands browsers respond to, may become unnecessary as web authoring programs become more common. In the meantime, though, it is worth learning some HTML. And some would argue that it will be worth knowing HTML even after it is not absolutely necessary. Knowing the underlying structure of anything can have its advantages, especially when problems occur. Someone who knows what is going on behind the scenes is often better prepared to discover solutions.

Most web servers run on UNIX workstations (though there are versions for many other operating systems as well). UNIX is a computer operating system that comes in a number of different versions, but most have some basic commands in common. In addition to learning HTML, you will need to know some of those UNIX commands in order to create directories and files that can be read by your web server. Specific procedures for creating web directories and for uploading and downloading files may vary from place to place, but the HTML code within each web document will be common to everyone.

13.2 Permissions

The first thing to do, in most cases, is create a directory named www in your UNIX account. The UNIX command is **mkdir www**, and it is entered at the system prompt.

For files to be visible to web users, the permissions have to be set correctly. "Permissions" refers to determining who has the ability to read a file, make changes to it, or execute it (executable files, usually programs, are files that do something when launched). The files that will make up your web pages should be set so that you have permission to read and write, the group has permission to read, and all others have permission to read. Because your web directory should also be set so that it is executable, it requires a slightly different command modifier.

To change files and directories, use the command chmod. For example, if I create a file called html_sample.html, I would need to set the permissions by typing at the system prompt **chmod 644 html_sample.html**. If I redisplay the directory (by typing **ls -al**), I should see in the file's permissions area:

-rw-r-- r--

The first hyphen (-) means this is a file, not a directory (if it were a directory, the string would read drw-r--r--). The following rw- refers to the permissions for you, the user. You can read the file and write new information in it. The first r-- refers to permissions for the group. Groups are defined groups of user ids. For example, at the University of Missouri, one group is all users with student accounts. Another group is users with faculty or staff accounts. In this case, anyone with a user id in your group will be able to read the file but will not be able to make any changes to it. The second r-- refers to permissions for anyone else, including the users who are not on your system. Again, anyone outside the group will be able to read the file but will not be able to write to it.

To correctly set the permissions on your web directory, type **chmod 755 www** when you are in your home directory. The result should look like this when you type **ls -al** (x indicates executable):

drwxr-xr-x

13.3   Introduction to HTML

Web documents are just text files, the kind that can be created with any word processor or text editor on just about any computer platform or operating system. What makes a text file a web document is the presence of hypertext markup language. To be more precise (since web browsers can also read plain text documents without HTML), HTML provides the means to create hypertext and hypermedia documents. HTML is what tells the web browser how to format the content of a file and where to take users who follow links.

Hypertext, by the way, refers to systems of organizing information associatively rather than sequentially. Books are fundamentally sequential in the way they organize information. They are designed to be read one page after another, one chapter after another, beginning to end. Hypertext allows you to jump from one place to another without following a preset sequence. That is, readers follow associations, or webs if you will, of meaning.

You are already familiar with a kind of hypertext if you've ever read a book that had an index. If you start at the beginning of the book, the table of contents maps out the sequence of information. If you start at the end, with the index, the order is alphabetical, and you choose specific bits of information based on the content you expect to find rather than by page sequence. You can leap around in the book if you use the index as your map. Hypertext software and systems like the Web mainly automate that "index" approach to reading.

HTML consists of a set of tags that provide instructions to web browsers viewing the document. Tags are simple codes enclosed in angle brackets (< >). There are instructions to the web browser telling it how to format the document or telling it how to find image files or documents at the other end of links. Most people are familiar with this process even though they don't often think about it. Consider a typical word processor. It has commands or menu choices that make text bold or italic, change the margins, increase font size, and so on. Each of these formatting features is controlled by tags, but in most word processors, the tags are invisible. They are embedded in the document so that the program can display text correctly, but out of the way of users as they create the document. With HTML, writers have to deal with the tags directly.

13.4 HTML Basics

All HTML files should end with .html or .htm following the filename. For example, the homepage for *RhetNet, A Cyberjournal for Rhetoric and Writing,* is index.html. Many HTML tags come in pairs, one to begin a formatting command and one to end the command. One of the most common errors new HTML writers make (the authors included) is to leave out an ending tag or fail to include the slash mark that differentiates the ending tag from the beginning tag.

Tags must be enclosed in angle brackets. For example, each document should begin with an <HTML> tag designating it as an HTML document. The ending tag, which in this case goes at the end of the document, is </HTML>.

Documents have two main parts, the head (<HEAD></HEAD>) and the body (<BODY></BODY>), which serve as containers for the contents of the file. The head element often contains only the document title tag though other special items can be used there.

The <TITLE></TITLE> tag holds the title of the window in which the document is displayed, so the text in the title tag will appear in the title bar of the browser window, not in the document itself. For that reason, titles are often short versions of the document's main heading.

Here's an example of the beginning of a typical HTML document:

```
<HTML>
<HEAD>
<TITLE>Sample HTML Document</TITLE>
</HEAD>
```

The body element contains all the things you see in the web page when it is displayed by a browser. The most common HTML features used in web pages are headings, paragraphs, lists, links, and images. There are many other possibilities, but knowing how to do these will be enough to get started.

<H> Headings

The <H> tag always includes a number from 1 to 6. <H1></H1> creates the dominant heading on the page, <H2></H2> is a bit smaller, <H3></H3> smaller yet, and so on. Note that the <H> tags do not refer to a specific font and size. They describe the size of the characters relative to the plain text in the document. The actual size and font may vary depending on the default setting of the browser or on changes users have made to their own copy of the browsers. For example, <H1> might be 24-point Palatino on my copy of Netscape, but it might be 20-point Geneva on MacWeb (or on someone else's copy of Netscape, for that matter).

<P> Paragraphs

The paragraph tag has long been one of the exceptions to the rule that tags come in pairs. <P> by itself is currently sufficient to separate paragraphs (<P> literally invokes a hard return followed by a line space).

\<L> Lists

There are several kinds of lists in HTML, but the most common are unordered list, \<UL>\</UL>, ordered list, \<OL>\</OL>, and definition list, \<DL>\</DL>. In the case of ordered and unordered lists, the items in the list are preceded by \<LI>, which is another tag that does not require a closing tag. Definition lists include two elements, the term to be defined, \<DT>, and the definition itself, \<DD>.

\<A HREF> Links

The \<HREF> (hypertext reference) tag links words or images into links to other places in the file or to other places on the Web. What falls between \<A HREF> and \</A> is the address of the destination for users following the link. There are shortcuts, but here we will include only the full version of the tag. The address should be a URL, so include the server address, the directory path, and the filename of the destination.

\<IMG SRC> Image Source

Several common image file formats are in use on the Web. These different formats are roughly analogous to the difference in format between documents created in different word processing programs, between Microsoft Word and WordPerfect, for instance. The most common and easiest-to-use image format is GIF. Others, especially JPEG, will work fine, but when you get started, you might want to convert any images you use to GIF format and make sure the filename ends with .gif. Not all graphics programs include GIF and JPEG as formats you can save files in, so if you get into web publishing much, you may want to find a conversion utility program, like GIFConverter, for the Macintosh. GIFConverter is a shareware program that converts standard formats like TIFF and PICT into GIF or JPEG (see http://www.kamit.com/gifconverter.html). This all looks like alphabet soup now, but these acronyms will become part of your vocabulary quickly if you do much web publishing, even if you do not know what they stand for.

The main reason to use GIF is that all graphic browsers can include GIF images inline, which means the images appear right in the window with the text. Netscape will do that with JPEG images, but many other graphic browsers still require a helper application to display a JPEG image, so the image appears in a new window.

For example, the logo for the Conference on College Composition and Communication, which appears on the organization's convention homepage (see http://www.missouri.edu/~cccc96/), has a filename of CCC.gif.

You don't have to possess image files in order to use them on your page, you just need to know the URL for their location on the Web. To find that, you can use the View Source command on graphic browsers to see the address in the <IMG SRC> tag of the image you want to use. It is very common to borrow HTML coding and image files from others on the Web. Be advised, though, that web authors may have copyright to some images, so it is safer and more courteous to write to a page author and ask for permission to use any image.

13.5 Sample HTML Document

You can use the following document as a template. Replace the text between the tags with your own information, put this document in a www directory on a machine with a web server, change the permissions, and you will have a web page of your own.

```
<HTML>
<HEAD>
<TITLE>Sample HTML</TITLE>
</HEAD>
<BODY>
<H1>This is a sample HTML page</H1>
<H2>This is a subhead sample</H2>
<P>
```

This is just a regular paragraph. Kind of boring.

```
<P>
```

This is a second paragraph. It's not much more interesting than the first one.

```
<P>
```

To spice things up a bit, we'll put a link to another site, to <A HREF=http://www.missouri.edu/~writery> The Online Writery</A>, an online writing and learning environment based at the University of Missouri. If you look at this document on the Web, the words *The Online Writery* will appear highlighted in some way, often with the color blue and underlining.

```
<UL>
<LI>This is an unordered list
<LI>Most browsers will interpret the "LI" tag as a bullet
<LI>You can make this list as long or short as you like
<LI>I've run out of items to put here, so I'm going to close
    this list
</UL>

<OL>
<LI>This is an ordered list
<LI>The main difference from the unordered list
<LI>Is that the "LI" tags are displayed as numbers: 1, 2, 3, etc.
</OL>

<DL>
<DT>Definition list
<DD>A definition list is a list that displays the term at the left
    margin and the definition about five spaces to the right.
<DT>This is another link to the <A
HREF=http://www.missouri.edu/~wleric/writery.html>Writery
    </A> is an example of a homepage using a definition list.
<DT>Another term
<DD>Another, much less interesting, definition
</DL>

<P>
```

Here are two simple .gif files. Both are simple arrows that we drew using HyperCard. They aren't very pretty, but you're welcome to use them if you like.

```
<IMG SRC="http://www.missouri.edu/~wleric/rtarrow.gif">
<IMG SRC="http://www.missouri.edu/~wleric/lftarrow.gif">

</BODY>
</HTML>
```

To see what this page looks like on the Web, access your local web browser and type in the following URL: **http://www.marlboro.edu/~nickc/vrpr/ericsamp.html.**

13.6   Basic UNIX Commands

As you can see by now from our combined FTP examples from Chapters 7 and 8, as well as the recent examples for writing your own web pages, knowing a little bit of UNIX helps a great deal when moving about on the Internet. You won't need this often, but we include these basic commands here for when you do.

Remember that UNIX is case sensitive. A file called send-money.txt is different from Sendmoney.txt. For this reason, if you name files when saving to a UNIX system, choose names that are long enough to let you know what is in the file, but also short enough to minimize the chance of error in managing the file. UNIX allows filenames to be up to thirty characters long. Using eight or so characters plus a three-character extension (similar to DOS for PCs) should be a workable length.

HELPFUL HINT: When saving software files to a UNIX account before downloading it to your own computer, it is best not to change the name or extensions of the file. Often a software file may have more than one extension, for example, untaranduncompress.sit.hqx. We recommended saving it that way so that when it is downloaded to your computer, you know exactly what software you will need to decompress it. In this case, StuffIt Expander would decompress the Bin-Hex (.hqx) first, and the StuffIt (.sit) next, with one command. To avoid errors in downloading, you can use a wildcard in UNIX. Thus, if you were using zmodem protocol to download the file, you could type **sz untar*** at your prompt. This will download any file beginning with the name *untar*.

Basic UNIX Commands

ls	Lists files and subdirectories in your current directory.
ls -l	Lists files and subdirectories, shows their size, last date they were modified, and the user rights assigned to them.
ls -la	Lists everything indicated with ls -l, as well as files and subdirectories beginning with a period. Most files and directories that begin with a period are for working in the background with programs.

cd	Changes a directory.
cdup	Used in FTP servers to move back one directory.
cd ..	Used in UNIX accounts to move back one directory (note the space between cd and ..).
chmod	Changes the modification or user rights for files and directories. chmod works by "totaling" the array of rights you wish to assign to a file.
cp	Copies a file. To copy test.txt to testback.txt, you would type **cp test.txt testback.txt.**
mkdir	Makes a directory. To create a directory called hold, you would type **mkdir hold.** You can then type **cd hold** to go into it.
mv	Renames a file. To change the name of the file called test3.txt to testpass, you would type **mv test3.txt testpass.**
pwd	Shows you which directory you are in.
rm	Removes files. Be careful not to type *, which is a UNIX wildcard. The command **rm *** will remove all files in a directory, including files that are essential to logging in and operating software if they are in that directory. If you want to remove a number of files, but not all, the command **rm -i*** will prompt you for a yes or no before each file, allowing you to work through the directory quickly. Be careful not to type **y** when you mean **n**.
rmdir	Removes a directory. To remove the directory called hold, you would type **rmdir hold.** A directory must be empty of files before it can be removed with this command. Use **rm-r** to delete a directory and its contents.

14

Plagiarism, Copyright, and the Internet

14.1 Introduction

Teachers, as you know, are concerned about plagiarism. It is viewed as one of the worst academic sins anyone can commit. Every English handbook includes a chapter on citing sources, on how to avoid plagiarism by knowing the difference between paraphrasing, summarizing, and quoting. Every student handbook we've seen details the academic penalties for plagiarism. Most introductory college writing courses require students to write a term paper, and to use and document outside sources. Many such courses include a tour of the school library to get an overview of how to use its resources.

In this section of the book, we offer an overview of the Internet that invites you to think of it as an *electronic library* where you can find and use a seemingly inexhaustible array of resources. As you read through this section, keep in mind your school's or English teacher's definition of plagiarism and the standards that your institution has adopted. Even if you haven't learned them yet, dig out your student handbook or English handbook and review it. You want to keep those standards in mind as you conduct research on the Internet.

14.2   The Difference Between Paper and Pixels

Libraries have been part of academic culture for thousands of years. As students, you learn to turn to books for knowledge; you are taught how to take notes from them, how to study them, and how to recall and use what you have read in them. The importance of books is in part tied to their permanence. Once a book is printed and bound, it can be used again and again. This ability for a book to circulate, to be read more than once, is what makes libraries and scholarship possible.

One reason academia places so much emphasis on citing a source correctly is so that when someone reads the essay in which a source is cited, he or she can use the citation to go to a library and get the exact book or article the author cited. Perhaps you have done research this way already, by using the bibliography of one book or article as a way to find more information on a subject. This tool of scholarship works so well because the researcher is confident that he or she will be able to read the same work, in the same form (or edition in bibliographical terms), that the author did. Reading an article in full allows the scholar to better judge it. The beauty of print is that it is fixed and therefore fairly reliable.

The Internet is not a print library. It comes to you in pixels, the individual dots on your computer screen that combine to form letters, words, and images. Unlike print, pixels are very fluid. They can be changed, moved, deleted, and copied with a few keystrokes. This fluidity offers both exciting advantages and some serious concerns for researchers working on the Internet.

14.3   Three Serious Concerns

Unfortunately for students, plagiarism is an overextended term. It is used to describe a variety of flaws, from an unintentional error in paraphrasing a source to the sad practice of how some students will "borrow" another student's essay and pass it off as their own. The first is a natural mistake in the learning process, one that is inevitably going to occur in every classroom given the complexity of learning how to paraphrase correctly. The other is fraud, and sometimes even theft.

One concern we have heard is that students might be tempted by the ease with which an essay from the Internet can simply be copied and pasted, in part or in whole, into a student's file and then handed in as the work of the student. People are concerned students will be tempted to fraud and theft.

A second concern of researchers and teachers about sources found on the Internet is their stability. Will they be there tomorrow, and if they are, will they be the same version as they were the day before? The Internet is in constant flux. Some sources are new forms: archived e-mail discussions, logs of MOO meetings, collaborative hypertext essays. Do these deserve the same stature as a rigorously written article appearing in a highly regarded academic journal?

A third concern, one for writers who put their work online to consider, is the difference between plagiarism and copyright violation. A student may hand in a paper that analyzes a poem he or she read in *The New Yorker* magazine. In so doing, the student might very well include the full text of the poem and would no doubt cite it correctly, giving full credit and bibliographical information about the poem. He or she will easily satisfy all the rules for academic citing and will not have committed plagiarism. In the traditional classroom where a paper is read only by fellow students and a teacher, the inclusion of the full text of the poem is not a problem. However, if the student puts the essay on the Internet, perhaps as part of a collection of class essays, the poem will in effect be published. It will be available to anyone on the Internet — millions of potential readers. *The New Yorker* and the poet face a possibility of lost revenues because a poem they are trying to sell is now available for nothing. Thus, in this example, though the use of the poem would not be plagiarism, it would be a copyright violation.

14.4   Concern One: Honesty

Teachers and students both should be concerned about the fraud and theft of another writer's words. It is wrong to pass off the work of another as one's own, no matter what technology is used to complete the crime. Before digital technology and electronic files, students and established authors simply rewrote or retyped the already printed words of others with whatever writing technology was at hand: quill, pen, or typewriter. (Yes, students are not the only people to steal ideas and words. See Thomas Mallon's excellent history and overview of plagiarism, *Stolen Words: Forays into the Origins and Ravages of Plagiarism,* New York: Ticknor and Fields, 1989.) People who decide to cheat and steal will not be stopped by returning to an older technology. Technology does not determine integrity.

Consider the complexities of collaboration

Although it is wrong to steal, keep in mind that the Internet can encourage both planned collaboration and learning and thinking by osmosis. When collaboration is planned, students and teachers can arrange ways to keep track of who does what and how to evaluate it. However, some collaboration occurs just from bringing people together. Consider, for example, that in e-mail discussions it is not unusual to absorb an idea into one's own writing and thinking. A student may pick up on an idea mentioned in a message and expand on it in her own message; she may be asked a question about her expansion that makes her rethink and refine it. After her refinement, another writer might add a new twist to the idea. The student might take the new twist and add it to her evolving sense of the idea. She might save a copy of the message that sums up her final position and download it to use in an essay. That downloaded message represents the work of three or four people; the student acted as a synthesizer and editor (as did the others in the discussion), borrowing ideas and reshaping them in light of new ideas.

To our minds, and this is what we recommend to our students, the student in this scenario would not be plagiarizing if she used any of her messages, including the downloaded one summing up her final position, a position obviously influenced by other writers. The ideas in question, even the words in question, cease to be the intellectual property of this or that writer. In the give and take of the discussion, as words are shared and merged, participating earns the writer the right to the words that emerge. However, keep in mind that if the student downloads another author's e-mail message, she must cite that.

Keep a writing portfolio and research log

Many teachers wisely advise students to save all the writing they do while drafting an essay, everything from first notes and brainstorming ideas, to drafts, to feedback notes from those who read the essay for you. Some teachers will ask you to keep journals to reflect on your writing or to keep track of your research. If you decide to use the Internet for research, using these ideas — keeping drafts and making reflective writing and reading journal entries — will show that any essay you hand in has evolved from your own work.

Use mixed fonts

Another way to address concerns about the malleability of electronic sources is to make sure you do not mix a source's words into your own in the drafting process. Use the computer to help you see what words are yours and what words are a source's by using different fonts. For example, you might write your words in `courier 12-point font`, and save the text from any of your download sources in a font that is starkly different, say, perhaps **helvetica 14-point bold font**.

> HELPFUL HINT: Earlier we mentioned the complexity of paraphrasing. If you consult an English writing handbook, you'll see that the key to paraphrasing is accurately mixing your words with another author's. This means you have to be diligent about where you place quotation marks and footnotes or references. By using for your text a font different from that used for your source's text, you'll give yourself a visual aid when paraphrasing. As part of your final draft proofreading, simply put quotes around the paraphrased text. And don't forget to convert all fonts to the same font when your documentation and quotation marks are in place.

14.5   Concern Two: Stability and New Forms of Scholarship

Stability is a harder concern to address because so much of the Internet is not stable. However, there are safeguards a researcher can use to help assure that those who read his or her work will be able to find the sources cited.

Brand names

One safeguard is to look for sources that come with a brand name. For example, *Time* magazine maintains a presence on the Internet (http://www.timeinc.com). If an English student were writing an essay on Jane Austen's *Sense and Sensibility,* and wanted to refer to how movie reviewers commented on the difference between the novel and the film, using the *Time* web page to access a review would not be a problem because Time Inc. has made a commitment to being online. Of course, there's no way of telling which publishers will stay on the Internet, but generally speaking, brand names are a useful indicator of permanence. Brand names do not mean, by the way, only commercial enterprises. Different academic groups maintain constant Internet presences, and often they are sponsored or affiliated with a college or university. Thus, for example, sources found on Carnegie Mellon University's English Server (http://englishserver.hss.cmu.edu/), which are vast and eclectic, are likely to be relatively stable.

Personal addresses

Look to see if an address includes a ~ with a name. For example, addresses for Nick's pages at Marlboro College all begin http://www.marlboro.edu/~nickc/. An address such as this means that the person whose name appears after the ~ is affiliated with the institution that runs the server indicated in the beginning of the address. These types of addresses will, as a general rule, be more temporary and subject to change than ones with paths directly to institutionally sponsored information.

Yes, but what about stability?

You'll notice qualifiers in the paragraphs preceding this one: "as a *general* rule," "increases the *chance*." We couldn't exactly give you a stable answer. Simply put, there is no stability. Not yet. Perhaps not for a long time, at least not any kind of stability that print enjoys. Print and publishing is an industry; there are financial interests (in academe, authors are paid with appointment, promotion, and tenure; thus the phrase *publish or perish*) that have helped solidify, over time, procedures for citing and documenting printed sources. Print sources also are stable. Journals and magazines and publishers come and go, but once something is printed, it is fixed; if it is reprinted, it is given a new edition number, or an editor will include a note telling you where it had been printed before. Print is fixed; pixels are fluid. That won't change.

Eventually, scholars will adjust to the fluidity of the Internet, and those who write online regularly will learn methods for saving their work and marking updates and additions. In fact, the Online Computer Library Center (OCLC, go to http://ora.rsch. oclc.org/oclc/menu/t-home1.htm) is working out ways to catalog Internet resources so that when you use an OCLC computer in your campus library to view its catalog of books, you'll be able to also get Internet references. In the meantime, when you question if a source will be there for another scholar to use, save the work on a diskette. If someone reads what you wrote and can't connect to the source you cited, he or she can always contact you, and you can e-mail the person a copy of what you used.

Journals and peer review

When searching for an online academic journal to use in your research, one aspect important to many scholars is whether the journal is peer reviewed. In peer-reviewed journals, an author submits an essay for consideration. The journal's editor sends copies of the essay to other scholars in the same field as the essay's subject addresses. These scholars read the essay to make sure its research is up to date and accurate, to see if it is well written and properly documented, and to judge whether it is timely and offers ideas of value to the scholarly community it addresses. For this reason, journals that are peer reviewed are usually regarded as worthy sources (both on the Internet and in print). However, as useful as peer review is (it's helped enormously with this book), scholars are using new ways to build knowledge.

New kinds of academic excellence

A good researcher should not limit himself or herself to just those sources that have a brand name, academic affiliation, or peer review publication procedure. For example, many journals are experimenting with nonpeer-reviewed submissions. Others are making use of genres available only on the Internet: symposia carried out by e-mail, MOOs used to do presentations for academic conferences, or collaborative essays and hyperfiction. These new forms for scholarship are radically different from the traditional vehicle of the published-in-print paper or book. Instead of reading an article by a sole author, the Internet may present you with a multisided perspective on an issue.

14.6   Concern Three: Plagiarism Meets Copyright

Digital technology is premised on copying. Every time you call up a file to your screen, you are calling up a copy of the original file as it resides on someone's computer. If you send a friend the file, you are not sending him or her your copy of the file, you are sending him or her a copy of your copy of the file. This ability to copy work — whether the file is digitized words, music, graphics, or moving pictures — has led many people and organizations to call for restrictions on sharing electronic information. Right now there is a controversy on how to balance the rights of authors and publishers to protect their work versus the rights of others to access and duplicate it.

For now, however, we'd like to turn to a more immediate practicality. If you do place an essay on the Internet, you could be subject to and held accountable for copyright provisions as described in the scenario where a student writes an analysis of a *New Yorker* poem. Although the chances of a student's class assignment attracting much attention on the Internet is low, considering all the information out there, students and teachers who work online should follow the same guidelines on copyright that publishers use.

Material in the public domain may be quoted freely. Many electronic text archives, such as those maintained by Project Gutenberg (http://jg.cso.uiuc.edu/PG/welcome.html), are composed of works in the public domain. Authors hold a copyright on their work for their lifetime. Their heirs or publishers can keep the copyright for another fifty years. Fifty years after the death of the author, the material is considered to be in the public domain.

For quoting from copyrighted works, use the following rules of thumb:

1. You can quote excerpts of 300 words from a book or 150 words from a magazine or newspaper article if the following conditions are met:

    The excerpt is not a complete unit in the larger work from which you found it, such as a poem in a magazine, a chapter in a book, an article in a newspaper, or a list of rules in a manual.

    The excerpt makes up less than 20 percent of the total words in your source document.

    The excerpted words are integrated into your essay and do not stand alone as an anthology or chapter opening.

    You give full credit to the author, source, and publisher.

2. If you quote several short quotations from a source, and the total more than 300 words for a book or 150 words for a

magazine or newspaper, you must get permission to use the quote.

3. You should get permission for using e-mail messages, including those you find in Usenet, and unpublished writing such as personal letters sent to you, diary entries, and classmates' essays. Because poems are usually smaller units within larger works, you should get permission for more than four lines or 20 percent of the poem, whichever is greater.

These are the publishing industry's current standards for judging fair use and getting copyright permissions. They are offered only as a guideline and do not, of course, represent a legal definition or legal advice. Each book you use will indicate who holds the copyright on the work in the book. You will usually find that information on the title page. If a book quotes another work, you might also see a separate acknowledgment on the copyright page; these acknowledgments will give you names you can look up to get addresses on. You can write to copyright holders to request permission. It is best when doing so to let the copyright holder know why you are writing, how you plan to use the copyrighted work, and where it will be appearing online. For example, if you hand in a class essay, it might be online for only one semester. If you submit a poetry review to an online literary magazine, it could be there indefinitely. These differences may be important to the copyright holder.

If you decide to quote lengthy excerpts from works you find online, they will often include an e-mail address that belongs to the copyright holder; this makes it easy to write for permission. E-mail is an example of copyrighted work (it is automatically copyrighted) for which you need permission; other essays you find online should be checked for permission. One advantage to using online sources, especially if you are working in the Web, is that you can easily include a link to the source. Many people who contribute online work will place a message in their work that declares the extent and type of copyright they hope to enforce. A common one reads, "This work may be redistributed freely, in whole or in part, but cannot be sold or used for profit or as part of a product or service that is sold for profit."

Remember, you need permission only to quote the copyrighted *words* of others. We will not get into the sticky subject of using copyrighted images and music. Just keep in mind that ideas cannot be copyrighted; only the expression (the particular arrangement of words) an author uses can be copyrighted. Thus you can summarize and restate any work in your own words. However, as you know from referring to an English handbook, when you do summarize, you must still cite the source so that you do not commit plagiarism.

Evaluating web sites: a list of guides

Since the first edition of this book, a number of web sites have been written by librarians and English teachers that offer visitors' guides and advice in evaluating World Wide Web information. Here is a brief list of the best guides we have found.

Teaching Critical Evaluation Skills for World Wide Web Resources

By Jan Alexander and Marsha Tate at the Wolfgram Memorial Library at Widener University. This is one of the first and best guides.

http://www.science.widener.edu/~withers/webeval.htm

Thinking Critically About World Wide Web Resources

By Esther Grassian, UCLA College Library. This is a page of very good questions to ask about sources. Save a copy for class discussions.

http://www.library.ucla.edu/libraries/college/instruct/
critical.htm

Online Writing Support Center: Using Cybersources

By Nancy L. Stegall of DeVry Institute of Technology. This is very thorough and has links to a range of other sites (including some listed here). It is a good one to start with.

http://www.devry-phx.edu/lrnresrc/dowsc/integrty.htm

Evaluating Quality on the Net

By Hope Tillman, Library Director at Babcock College. This is very detailed, with links to examples and comparisons with print-based standards.

http://www.tiac.net/users/hope/findqual.html

Evaluating Internet Research Sources

Robert Harris, an English teacher at Southern California College. This is a well-wrought and smart essay; we recommend you read it before starting your research.

http://www.sccu.edu/faculty/R_Harris/evalu8it.htm

For more information on evaluating Internet sources and on copyright, visit the *Writing Online* web site. You're welcome to post specific questions that we can try to answer in our research forum.

15

Citing Internet Sources

15.1 Tips on Creating Correct Citations

Electronic sources are growing faster than scholars can find conventions for citing them, so you might easily find a source for which there is no sample entry. Therefore, keep the following tips in mind.

Be consistent with other citations

If you can't find a citation example, use your best judgment and be consistent. The punctuation used to separate the elements of your citation (author's name, document title, source, date, and so on), and the elements' order, should be consistent with other citations.

Don't be afraid to give too much information

Remember you are citing both to credit your source and to allow interested readers the complete information they will need to

111

find the source for themselves. It is better to err, then, in providing too much information rather than not enough.

Consider using explanatory footnotes when needed

Since you are working with new media, you might need to include explanatory footnotes about the sources. See section 15.7 for an example.

15.2   Working with Files Accessed from the Internet

Keep careful records

You should make sure you record the following information when you access an Internet source.

1. The means of access: WWW, telnet, FTP, e-mail, and so on.
2. The address and path used to reach the resource.
3. The status of the document. Some documents evolve over time; they will usually indicate that they do; look for a version number or the date of most recent update.
4. The date on which you access the piece.

A special note on downloading files

Some files must be downloaded onto your own computer to be read. For example, many documents are stored in a particular word processing format. When you download a document of this type, include in your citation the software format and version number (for example, CommonSpace 2.1) of the file. Use the page numbers as they appear when you first open the file in the designated word processor.

15.3   Citation Guidelines

Most English literature and writing journals favor the Modern Language Association (MLA) in-text citation method. Some require the American Psychological Association (APA) in-text citation method. And a few will ask for papers to be done according to *The Chicago Manual of Style* (CMS). In this section, we will show you examples of how to cite Internet sources using all three styles.

A note on MOO and MUD conversations

With computers, it is very easy to log your online activity. Logs will capture and save everything you see on screen, including commands, error messages, text you write, and comments written by someone else in a discussion. Most MOO, MUD, and IRC clients include a log feature. There are many legitimate reasons to log what you do, and you don't have to announce every time you are logging. However, you should never quote a player's remarks or e-mail from a MOO or MUD without permission or prior arrangement; to quote without permission is unethical. A participant in a MOO or MUD (see Chapter 11) is called a player. In MOOs and MUDs, people are known first by their player names, and second, if at all, by their full real names. If you know or can learn a player's real name, use it in parenthesis if it's important and you have permission to do so. For planned interviews and arranged meetings, prefer the real name in the citation unless your research criteria or subject matter call for an alias. If you use a player name or other alias in an arranged interview, make sure you note why you are doing so in your paper. Always keep a log for a planned interview.

15.4 Modern Language Association (MLA) Style Guidelines

In the first edition of this book, we relied on the work of Janice R. Walker of the University of South Florida. She was the first person to present a systematic use of the MLA style for citing electronic sources. Recently, however, the MLA has released their own official recommendations for citing Internet sources (*MLA Style Manual and Guide to Scholarly Publishing, second edition*). While this section now reflects the current MLA guidelines, note that the MLA focused on "sources for which a considerable amount of relevant publication information is available" (210) and favored "refereed, authoritative sources" (211). We offer some additional examples of sources not covered by the MLA. These represent our best attempts to apply the MLA's principles.

Creating a work-cited entry

The principles involved in these citations are straightforward and consistent. Here's the order of elements for the work-cited entry:

1. Author's full name, last name first.
2. "Title of article" (for articles in journals, magazines, or anthologies).
3. Title of publication (for journals, magazines, books, or anthologies).
4. Volume number, issue number, or version number, if given.
5. Date published, if given.
6. Length (in page, paragraph, or section numbers), if given.
7. Date of access and URL.

The MLA offers examples for material accessed via the WWW, and therefore only shows examples that use a URL. If you access information by something other than a WWW browser, follow steps 1–6, skip 7, then follow steps 8–11.

8. Date accessed by you.
9. Internet protocol (e.g., MOO, Telnet, FTP).
10. Internet address and path.
11. Special instructions if applicable (e.g., "@go room" in a MOO).

Working citations into your text

Most of the time when you use the MLA, you will use parentheses in the text of your essay to tell a reader that you're referencing something. The parentheses will include an author's last name and the page number for the reference: (name #). If your Internet source indicates page numbers, you are fine. If they number paragraphs or screens, you should write your citation like so: (name par. #). If they do not number paragraphs or screens, you can count them. This can be tricky and exhausting for long pieces, however. Therefore, an acceptable option is to use the abbreviation n. pag for no pagination: (name n. pag).

MLA style for e-mail

Personal e-mail

Give the author's name (if known), the subject line from the posting in quotation marks, and note that it is personal mail. The date refers to date of the message. Since e-mail does not come with page breaks, you do not need to note that it has no pagination in your in-text citation.

Pleiske, Mary. "Teaching About AIDS." (24 April 1994). E-
mail to author. .

E-mail from a discussion list, archived

For mail from an archived list, begin with the author's name, followed by the subject line in quotes. Next, use the decriptor *Online posting*, the date the message was posted, and the name of
the e-mail list archives. (Note: If you use the word "archives" in
the title, it will make the nature of the URL clearer to your readers. Close with the date you read the message, followed by the
URL in angle brackets.

Wood, Wini. "Re: Alliance Gopher standards (FWD)." Online
posting. 17 July 1994. Alliance for Computers and Writing List (ACW-L) Archives. 25 August 1995.
<http://www.ttu.edu/lists/acw-l/9407/0017.html>.

E-mail for a discussion list, nonarchived

After the writer's name and message title, use the descriptor
Online posting followed by the date posted, the name of the e-
mail list, the date you read the message, and in angle brackets
the URL to a web site associated with the list. If the e-mail list
has no web site, use the e-mail address for the owner or moder-
ator of the list.

Earnshaw, Catherine. "Oh What Heights We'll Hit." 1 April
1998. Rhetnet, A Cyberjournal for Rhetoric and Writing
Discussion List. 4 April 1998. <http://www.missouri.
edu/~rhetnet/>.

File requested from an e-mail program

TESLEJ-L refers to the name of the list the file is on. It serves to
the filename as a journal title does to an article title. Give both
the list management address (it's the address you send the commands to) and the command that must be sent in order to request and receive the cited file.

Corio, Ron, Sokolik, M., & Lee, A. "APA Style Guide," ver 2.1.
Online posting. March 1995 TESLEJ-L. 18 April 1995.
<listserv@cmsa.berkeley.edu, send message: Get
TESLEJ-L APAGUIDE TESLEJ-L F=Mail>

E-mail from a usenet group

Usenet posts may be posted on one day, but not read by you until later. Therefore include the date posted first, then your date of access next. To indicate the posting is from Usenet, place in angle brackets the prefix *news:* followed by the group name.

> Twain, Mark. "Re: Rumors of My Death." Online posting. 10 September 1995. 13 September 1995. <news:misc.writing>.

MLA style for file transfer protocol (FTP)

You'll note in this example for Brendan Kehoe's "Zen and the Art of the Internet," which we recommend, that a revision number is given by the author. Note also that the FTP address (ftp.internic.net) and the directory path (pub/Internet-doc/zen.txt) are separated by a comma. Writing it this way indicates that the file was accessed by using the file transfer protocol directly, as described in Chapter 7.

> Kehoe, Brendan. "Zen and the Art of the Internet: A Beginner's Guide to the Internet," rev. 1.0. 2 February 1992. 2 March 1994. <ftp.internic.net, pub/Internet-doc/zen.txt>.

Here's how the same citation would look if it were accessed via the WWW.

> Kehoe, Brendan. "Zen and the Art of the Internet: A Beginner's Guide to the Internet," rev. 1.0. 2 February 1992. 2 March 1994. <ftp://ftp.internic.net/pub/Internet-doc/zen.txt>.

MLA style for the World Wide Web

This will be your most commonly used citation. The WWW, because it can activate gopher, FTP, telnet, e-mail, Usenet, and other protocols, is the most widely used Internet interface. Although in the popular mind the WWW equals the Internet, technically, that's not true, and there are still a number of ways to use the Internet without using the WWW. It's easy to see when another protocol is being used because the name of the protocol will replace the term *http*.

Slade, Robert M. "Book Review: Netiquette by Virginia Shea." Computer Mediated Communication Magazine. October 1994. 15 September 1994. <http://sunsite.unc.edu/CMC/mag/1994/oct/netiquette.html>.

In the next example, give the term defined as the article and list the dictionary's site author as editor. The second date is your date of access. If the dictionary is searchable, as in this case, give the URL to the main page. The term defined is the search term that your reader would use.

"Laser." The ACRONYMs Dictionary. Ed. David Sill. 15 February 1993. 3 June 1995. <gopher://info.mcc.ac.uk:70/11/miscellany/acronyms>.

MLA style for MOOs, MUDs, and other telnet sites

Remember, you should never quote a player's remarks or e-mail from a MOO or MUD without permission or prior arrangement; to quote without permission is unethical. In all MOO or MUD citations, underline the name of the MOO or MUD.

MOO or MUD e-mail distribution list

MOOs or MUDs may have e-mail programs that allow personal e-mail and e-mail discussion lists. For author, give the player name. When a message comes from a list, provide the name of the list as well as the name of the MOO.

Mehitabel. "When I Ruled the Nile." Online posting. 10 July 1993. Governance List in SomeMOO. 14 July 1993. <telnet moo.somemoo.com 7777>.

Mail within a MOO or MUD

Even though the mail is to you, give the date it is written and the date you accessed it. Because you must go to a MOO to get the mail, the date of access is important.

Traveler (Jones, Tom). "No Room at the Inn." Online posting. 22 August 1995. E-mail to author in SomeMOO. 24 August 1995. <telnet: moo.somemoo.com 7777>.

MOO/MUD writings

To show you how to cite a document in a MOO, we use an example from our imaginary MOO. After the telnet address for the MOO, you should give, and separate by commas, the series of commands needed to get to the document.

> Pirate (Hawkins, Jim). "Welcome to My Island." 5 December 1992. SomeMOO. 3 January 1993. <telnet moo. somemoo.com 7777, @go silver's_lair, read welcome>.

Nonplanned discussion

> Pirate (Hawkins, Jim). Remark made in SomeMOO. Internet. Telnet: moo.somemoo.com 7777, @go castaway beach (4 July 1994).

Planned interview

> Pirate (Hawkins, Jim). Personal interview conducted in SomeMOO. 4 July 1994. <telnet: moo.somemoo.com 7777, @go castaway beach, read interview>.

Discussion from a public log

Some MOO and MUD meetings are logged and archived, such as class meetings, planning sessions for collaborative projects, and scholarly discussions. Usually if there's a log, there's a title associated with the meeting. Make sure you note that in your reference. In the following example, the title is the name of the class. Note that the directions to the log are given and not the directions to the MOO. There's a date for the archive document and a second date for when you accessed it.

> Pirate (Hawkins, Jim). Class meeting for "English 341: Sea Fictions." 9 September 1994. SomeMOO: Melville Room. 1 September 1995. <http://www.somemoo.com/logs/ english/melville/090994.txt>.

Telnet to an online database

More and more databases are coming online and are available through the Internet. Some, such as the *Oxford English Dictionary* or *InfoTrak,* are licensed, and only students who attend the college or university that holds the license can access them. Other databases, however, are accessible online. You'll recall from Chapter 6 that we accessed Harvard's Online Library Information Service (HOLLIS). HOLLIS allows you to search the Educational Resources Information Center (ERIC) database.

The citation begins as it would were you citing a paper found via ERIC directly, including the database document details (ED number) for the paper. After that, name the service you used (HOLLIS) to learn about the paper, and how you accessed the service (telnet: 128.103.151.247 3006). You do not need to give your date of access. Spell out HOLLIS—it is not common enough to abbreviate, but you can abbreviate ERIC.

> Daisley, Margaret. "A Letter to My Mother." Paper presented at the National Council of Teachers of English Annual Meeting, Louisville, KY. 18-23 November 1992. ERIC, ED 355549. <u>Harvard Online Library Information Service.</u> <telnet 128.103.151.247 3006>.

15.5 American Psychological Association (APA) Style Guidelines

The groundwork for developing our sample APA guidelines came from Ron Corio and Maggi Sokolik who, with help from Abraham Lee, wrote APA guidelines for the online journal *Teaching English as a Second Language — Electronic Journal*. In addition, we followed their lead in consulting the work of Nancy Crane and Xia Li, whose book, *Electronic Styles: A Handbook for Citing Electronic Information* (Medford, NJ: Information Today, 1996), includes guidelines for both the MLA and APA styles. Crane and Li's work can be previewed on the WWW (http://www.uvm.edu/~ncrane/estyles/). For fuller details, consult an English handbook, most of which offer thorough APA coverage. APA citation elements follow this order:

1. Last name of author, followed by first initial (full first names only used if two authors in one citation have both the same last name and the same first initials).
2. Date, in parentheses, followed by a period.
3. Article titles are given without quotation marks or underlining. Book titles are underlined. The APA capitalizes only the first words of these titles, the first word of subtitles, and proper names within them.

4. The titles of journals and magazines are underlined and follow standard capitalization.
5. For books, after the title comes the place of publication followed by a colon, then the name of publisher to end the citation.
6. For journals and magazines, the page numbers come after the journal title and volume and issue information to end the citation.

To illustrate these by example, here's an APA entry for a book:

Katsh, E. A. (1989). The electronic media and the transformation of law. New York: Oxford University Press.

And here's an APA entry for an article in a journal:

Diegmuller, K. (1995, September). Expletives deleted. Teacher Magazine, 24-29.

The APA frowns on citing sources that others cannot access. Thus for unarchived e-mail or MOO meetings, mention them in text informally and not for major points: "In a discussion on SomeMOO, CarrotTop said salads give him the shivers." If you want to cite e-mail sent to you, and you think it might be important for other researchers to have access to the full content of the e-mail, you need to get permission from the sender to save a copy and make it available to those who write you about it.

APA style for e-mail

APA for citing personal e-mail

Crane and Li have done an excellent job of devising a simplified e-mail format. In their guide, however, they recommend that you include both the sender's e-mail address and your e-mail address as recipient. Since permission is needed to quote the letter, it may be more forthcoming without also publishing the sender's e-mail address. If you hold a copy of the message, that should be enough, and people can e-mail you if they need to see the message.

Brooke, D. (1995, March 15). Mid-March hare: A recipe. E-mail to Nick Carbone (nickc@english.umass.edu).

Message or file from e-mail program

The word *Internet* in brackets is a more specific replacement of Crane and Li's recommendation of *Online*. The APA is still evolving their Internet guidelines; however, for other online sources, such as CD-ROMs, they name the medium. Naming the Internet names the medium more precisely than "online" and is more consistent, we believe, with APA practice. The more specific you can be, the better off your readers will be. In this example, TESLEJ-L is the name of the discussion list under which the guide is available. The list name is underlined because its relationship to the guide is the same as a journal's to an article. The date ending the citation is the access date. The APA has brief citation advice available on its web site (http://www.apa.org/journals/webref.html).

> Corio, R., Sokolik, M., & Lee, A. (1995, July). APA style guide, ver. 2.2. TESLEJ-L. [Internet]. E-mail: listserv@cmsa.berkeley.edu, message: Get TESLEJ-L APAGUIDE TESLEJ-L F=MAIL [17 May 1997].

E-mail message available from anaArchive

> Wood, W. (1994, July 17). Re: Alliance gopher standards (fwd). Alliance for Computers and Writing List (ACW-L) Archives. [Internet]. WWW: http://www.ttu.edu/lists/acw-l/9407/0017.html [25 August 1995].

E-mail from a Usenet group

Usenet posts can be read for a limited number of days after originally being posted to the group. How long depends upon the length of time your school keeps the post stored. If you are going to use a Usenet posting, make sure you save a copy right away.

> Twain, Mark. (1995, September 10). Re: rumors of my death. [Internet]. Usenet: misc.writing. Available from nickc@english.umass.edu [13 September 1995].

APA style for file transfer protocol (FTP)

This is for FTP done directly, as described in Chapter 7. For FTP done via the WWW, you would give a URL instead of separating the host from the path by a comma.

Kehoe, B.P. (1992, February 2). Zen and the art of the internet, 2nd. rev. [Internet]. FTP: quake.think.com, pub/etext/1992/Zen10.txt [2 March 1994].

APA style for the World Wide Web

Slade, R. M. (1994, October). Book review: Netiquette by Virginia Shea Computer Mediated Communication Magazine, 1:6. [Internet]. WWW: http://sunsite.unc.edu/CMC/mag/1994/oct/netiquette.html [23 March 1996].

APA style for MOOs and MUDs

E-mail from a player

For MOO mail in APA, always place the access date at the end, even if it's personal mail.

Traveler (Jones, T.) (1993, January 2). No room at the inn. Personal e-mail on SomeMOO. [Internet]. Telnet: moo.somemoo.com 7777. Available from nickc@english.umass.edu [3 January 1993].

E-mail from a MOO or MUD list

Note, even if you access a message on the same date it is sent, still give the access date.

Traveler (Jones, T.). (1993, March 3). I vote yes to a council. E-mail on Governance list in SomeMOO. [Internet]. Telnet: moo.somemoo.com 7777. Available from nickc@english.umass.edu [3 March 1993].

Files from a MOO

Always include the access date on which you read a file in a MOO (even if, as in the example, it's the same day the file was published). Include the MOO commands needed to reach the file.

Pirate (Hawkins, J.). (1993, January 2). Welcome to my island. File in SomeMOO, n. pag. [Internet]. Telnet: moo.somemoo.com 7777, @go silver's lair, read welcome [3 January 1993].

Interviews and meetings from a MOO

Pirate (Hawkins, J.). (1993, April 2). Interview in SomeMOO. [Internet]. Telnet: moo.somemoo.com 7777, @go silver's lair. Transcript available from nickc@english.umass.edu.

APA style for telnet to an online database

If you review the MLA entry on page 119 for telnet to an online database, you'll find a detailed explanation for the elements involved in this citation example.

Daisley, M. (1992, November 18-23). A letter to my mother. Paper presented at the National Council of Teachers of English Annual Meeting, Louisville, KY. [Internet]. Harvard Online Library Information Service. Telnet: 128.103.151.247 3006. ERIC, ED 355549.

15.6 *The Chicago Manual of Style* (CMS) Guidelines

The editors of the most recent (fourteenth) edition of *The Chicago Manual of Style* write that the "proliferation of documents created, stored, and disseminated on computer systems and the burgeoning requirement to cite such documents" means that creating "a uniform system of citing electronic documents" is still ongoing. The examples in this section are based upon our attempt to approximate *The Chicago Manual of Style* guidelines.

Most students who use the Chicago style refer to Kate L. Turabian's *A Manual for Writers of Term Papers, Theses, and Dissertations,* also published by the University of Chicago Press. You should refer to this book for more information, including details on the differences between the footnote and bibliography method and the in-text citation method for citing sources. We give examples for both methods.

In the Chicago style, the parenthetical reference includes the author, the date, and the page number; for example: (Crump and Carbone 1997, 7). Some Internet sources will provide page number equivalents; others will number paragraphs. If you cite a source that numbers paragraphs, note that in the citation: (Slade 1994, paragraph 3). If no page numbers or paragraph numbers are provided, you can choose either to count the paragraphs or to use the abbreviation n. pag for no pagination: (Smith 1996, n. pag).

In this edition, we've simplified how we approach the CMS guidelines. We treat the information for the author, date, and title of the work as it would appear in a print source, except for the caveat about capitalizing titles. For the portion of the citation that gives the Internet details, we try in each example to approximate the name of the web site or e-mail list with the title of a book, the word *Internet* with the publisher location, and the particular protocol and address with the name of the publisher.

Here's an overview by comparative templates, with the CMS for a print source first:

Footnotes

[1]First Last, "Title," In <u>Book Title</u>, ed. by Name, (Place: Publisher, Date), page.

[1]First Last, "Title," In <u>List or Web Site</u>, (Internet: Protocol: Address, Date), page reference (or n. pag).

Bibliography

Last, First. "Title." In <u>Book Title</u>. Ed. by Name. Place: Publisher, Date.

Last, First. "Title." <u>List or Web Site</u>. Internet: Protocol: Address, Date. Accessed on date (if needed). Available from userid@e-mail.address (if needed).

Works cited

Last, First. Year. Title. <u>Book title</u>, ed. by Name. Place: Publisher.

Last, First. Year. Title. <u>List or web site</u> (Month day) (if needed). Internet: Protocol: Address. Accessed on date (if needed). Available from userid@e-mail.address (if needed).

Computer information services and databases

When citing an article found through an electronic database such as ERIC that you reached via the Internet, you begin as though you had found it in the original source. Then you provide how you reached the database, followed by the database name and the identifying information the database assigns to the article. In the following example, that means using the Internet to telnet to Harvard's Online Library Information Service, choosing ERIC, and finding the document number (ED 355549) for Daisley's paper.

Footnote

[1]Margaret Daisley, "A Letter to My Mother," paper presented at the annual meeting of the National Council of Teachers of English, Louisville, KY, 18-23 November 1992, Harvard Online Library Information Service, Internet, Telnet: 128.103.151.247 3006, ERIC, ED 355549.

Bibliography

Daisley, Margaret. "A Letter to My Mother." Paper presented at the annual meeting of the National Council of Teachers of English, Louisville, KY, 18-23 November 1992. Harvard Online Library Information Service. Internet: Telnet: 128.103.151.247 3006. ERIC, ED 355549.

Work cited

Daisley, Margaret. 1992. A letter to my mother. Paper presented at the annual meeting of the National Council of Teachers of English, Louisville, KY, November 18-23. Harvard Online Library Information Service. Internet: Telnet: 128.103.151.247 3006. ERIC, ED 355549.

CMS style for e-mail

Remember, some distribution lists archive their messages, but many do not. Even if a list does maintain an archive, you would do well to save a full copy of a message you plan to cite, with all headers in place, on a disk, and be willing to make it available should someone request to see it. This will be a rare need, but it's worth keeping in mind. For all personal e-mail, you should provide your e-mail address.

Personal e-mail

Footnote

[1]Mary Pleiske, "Teaching About AIDS," (Internet: E-mail to author, 24 April 1994).

Bibliography

> Pleiske, Mary. "Teaching About AIDS." Internet: E-mail to author, 24 April 1994. Available from nickc@english. umass.edu.

Work cited

> Pleiske, Mary. 1994. Teaching about AIDS. Internet: E-mail to author, April 24. Available from nickc@english. umass.edu.

E-mail from a discussion list, nonarchived

Since this is nonarchived, you should save and have available a copy of the cited message. The list name should be underlined; it is to the message title what a magazine's title is to an article.

Footnote

> [1]Earnshaw, Catherine, "Oh What Heights We'll Hit," Rhetnet-L, (Internet: listproc@lists.missouri.edu, 1 April 1995).

Bibliography

> Earnshaw, Catherine. "Oh What Heights We'll Hit." Rhetnet-L. Internet: listproc@lists.missouri.edu, 1 April 1995. Available from nickc@english.umass.edu.

Work cited

> Earnshaw Catherine. 1995. Oh what heights we'll hit. Rhetnet-L. Internet: listproc@lists.missouri.edu, April 1. Available from nickc@english.umass.edu.

Archived e-mail

Footnote

> [1]Wini Wood, "Re: Alliance Gopher standards (FWD)," in Alliance for Computers and Writing List (ACW-L) Archives, (Internet: WWW: http://www.ttu.edu/lists/acw-l/9407/ 0017.html, 17 July 1994).

Bibliography

> Wood, Wini. "Re: Alliance Gopher standards (FWD)." From <u>Alliance for Computers and Writing List (ACW-L) Archives</u>. Internet: WWW: http://www.ttu.edu/lists/acw-l/9407/0017.html, 17 July 1994.

Work cited

> Wood, Wini. "Re: Alliance gopher standards (FWD). In <u>Alliance for Computers and Writing List (ACW-L) Archives</u> (July 17). Internet: WWW: http://www.ttu.edu/lists/acw-l/9407/0017.html.

Message or file from e-mail program

In this example, the date goes after the underlined list name; the list name is being treated like a journal title, and the date after it like a publication date.

Footnote

> [1]Ron Corio, Maggi Sokolik, & Abraham Lee, "APA STYLE GUIDE, ver. 2.1," on <u>TESLEJ-L</u> (July 1995), (Internet: E-mail: listserv@cmsa.berkeley.edu; message: get TESLEJ-L APAGUIDE TESLEJ-L F=MAIL).

Bibliography

> Corio, Ron, Sokolik, Maggi, and Lee, Abraham. "APA STYLE GUIDE, ver. 2.1." On <u>TESLEJ-L</u> (July 1995). Internet: E-mail: listserv@cmsa.berkeley.edu; message: get TESLEJ-L APAGUIDE TESLEJ-L F=MAIL. Accessed on 15 May 1997.

Work cited

> Corio, Ron, Sokolik, Maggi, and Lee, Abraham. 1995. APA STYLE GUIDE, ver. 2.1. On <u>TESLEJ-L</u> (July). Internet: E-mail: listserv@cmsa.berkeley.edu; message: get TESLEJ-L APAGUIDE TESLEJ-L F=MAIL. Accessed on 15 May 1997.

E-mail from a Usenet group

Footnote

> [1]Mark Twain, "Re: Rumors of My Death," on misc.writing, (Internet: Usenet, 31 October 1994).

Bibliography

> Twain, Mark. "Re: Rumors of My Death." On misc.writing. Internet: Usenet, 31 October 1994. Available from nickc@english.umass.edu.

Work cited

> Twain, Mark. 1994. Re: Rumors of my death. On misc. writing (October 31). Internet: Usenet. Available from nickc@english.umass.edu.

CMS style for citing from MOOs or MUDs

Personal e-mail sent inside a MOO or MUD

Footnote

> [1]Traveler (Tom Jones), "No Room at the Inn," E-mail to author in SomeMOO, (Internet: Telnet: moo.somemoo.com 7777, 24 August 1995).

Bibliography

> Traveler (Jones, Tom). "No Room at the Inn." E-Mail to author in SomeMOO. Internet: Telnet: moo.somemoo.com 7777, 24 August 1995. Available from nickc@english. umass.edu.

Work cited

> Traveler (Jones, Tom). 1995. No room at the inn. E-mail to author in SomeMOO (August 24). Internet: Telnet: moo.somemoo.com 7777. Available from nickc@english. umass.edu.

MOO or MUD e-mail distribution list

Sometimes within a MOO or MUD there are e-mail discussion groups. If a message comes from such a distribution list, include the name of the list and underline it.

Footnote

> [1]mehitabel, "When I Ruled the Nile," e-mail from Governance List in SomeMOO, (Internet: Telnet: moo.somemoo.com 7777, 14 July 1993).

Bibliography

> mehitabel. "When I Ruled the Nile." E-mail from Governance List in SomeMOO. Internet: Telnet: moo.somemoo.com 7777, 14 July 1993. Available from nickc@english. umass.edu.

Work cited

> mehitabel. 1993. When I ruled the Nile. E-mail from Governance List in SomeMOO (July 14). Internet: Telnet: moo.somemoo.com 7777. Available from nickc@english. umass.edu.

MOO or MUD discussion

Footnote

> [1]Painter (Dorian Gray), remark in SomeMOO: Artist Studio, (Internet: Telnet: moo.somemoo.com 7777; @go Artist Studio, 3 May 1993).

Bibliography

> Painter (Gray, Dorian). Remark in SomeMOO: Artist Studio. Internet: Telnet: moo.somemoo.com 7777; @go Artist Studio, 3 May 1993. Full transcript available from nickc@english.umass.edu.

In the work-cited entry, we'll show how you would cite this as a formal interview where the log is available online. Note how doing so changes what is significant. The path is to the log, not the MOO.

Work cited

> Gray, Dorian. 1993. Interview with author in SomeMOO: Artist Studio (May 30). Internet: WWW: http://www. umass.edu/~nickc/moo-logs/Gray.txt.

MOO and MUD papers

People can leave files in MOOs and MUDs for visitors to read. To cite a file, you must include the full set of MOO or MUD commands executed to reach the file after logging in. These must be presented in the same case (usually lowercase) you used to execute the command. Logging your MOO or MUD visits is a good way to make sure you record the commands accurately in your citation.

Footnote

[1]Pirate (Jim Hawkins), "Welcome to My Island," file in SomeMOO: Silver's Lair, (Internet: Telnet: moo. somemoo.com 7777; @go silver's lair; read welcome, no date given), n. pag.

Bibliography

Pirate (Hawkins, Jim). "Welcome to My Island." File in SomeMOO: Silver's Lair. Internet: Telnet: moo.somemoo. com 7777; @go silver's lair; read welcome, no date given. Accessed on 14 July 1996.

Work cited

Pirate (Hawkins, Jim). No date given. Welcome to my island. File in SomeMOO: Silver's Lair. Internet: Telnet: moo.somemoo.com 7777; @go silver's lair; read welcome. Accessed on 14 July 1996.

CMS style for file transfer protocol (FTP)

FTP is a way of logging onto a remote computer, moving among its storage space, choosing a file from it, and sending the file back to your own computer. The address in the example is for FTPing directly, as described in Chapter 7.

Footnote

[1]Brendan Kehoe, "Zen and the Art of the Internet: A Beginner's Guide to the Internet," rev. 1.0, (Internet: FTP: ftp. internic.net; path: pub/Internet-doc/zen.txt, 1992), paragraph 3.

Bibliography

> Kehoe, Brendan. "Zen and the Art of the Internet: A Beginner's Guide to the Internet," rev. 1.0. Internet: FTP: ftp.internic.net; path: pub/Internet-doc/zen.txt, 1992.

Work cited

> Kehoe, Brendan. 1992. Zen and the art of the internet: A beginner's guide to the internet, rev. 1.0. Internet: FTP: ftp.internic.net; path: pub/Internet-doc/zen.txt.

CMS style for the World Wide Web

For most of you, this will be the most common means of access. Note that for journals, CMS places the date after the journal title and volume information.

If you look closely at the footnote and bibliography examples, you'll notice that the footnote's URL ends with shatra.html and the bibliography's URL ends with shade.html. This is because the work being cited is a hypertext with more than one web page. The specific reference in the footnote is to content on the page reached by the URL ending in shatra.html. However, the work's starting web page begins at the URL given in the bibliography. The ability to designate a particular page in a hypertext is one advantage of the footnote and bibliography method.

Footnote

> [1]Leslie Regan Shade, "Balancing the Global Through the Local," Computer Mediated Communication Magazine, vol. 4, no. 2 (February 1997), (Internet: WWW: http://www. december.com/cmc/mag/1997/feb/shatra.html), n. pag.

Bibliography

> Shade, Leslie Regan. "Balancing the Global Through the Local." Computer Mediated Communication Magazine, vol. 4, no. 2 (February 1997). Internet: WWW: http://www. december.com/cmc/mag/1997/feb/shade.html.

Work cited

> Shade, Leslie Regan. 1997. Balancing the global through the local. Computer Mediated Communication Magazine,

vol. 4, no. 2 (February). Internet: WWW: http://www.
december.com/cmc/mag/1997/feb/shade.html.

15.7   Advice on Citing Hypertext Documents

Except for the last example in *The Chicago Manual of Style* section, all sample entries in this chapter have pointed to single
documents. However, there will be times on the Web when you
cite a hypertext, a piece with an array of interlinked pages. For
example, consider Doug Brent's *Kairos* hypertext, "Rhetorics of
the Web: Implications for Teachers of Literacy" (http://english.
ttu.edu/kairos/2.1/features/brent/wayin.htm). Brent's piece was
published in *Kairos,* volume 2, issue 1 (http://english.ttu.edu/
kairos/2.1). The hypertext contains sixty-one interlinked web
pages on the Kairos site. In addition to that, Brent's works-cited
page lists more than fifty works, approximately a third of which
are on the Web and have links to them, both from the works-
cited page itself and as needed within Brent's other pages.

If you quote or cite Brent, how do you accurately lead readers
to the correct page while giving the correct information for both
Kairos and the first page in Brent's piece? Here's what we suggest.
If you are using footnotes and bibliography as described by CMS,
follow the WWW example given in the CMS section for Leslie
Regan Shade's piece. That is, in the footnote put the URL to the
page being cited, and in the bibliography, put the URL to the first
page of the hypertext. You do not need a separate URL for the
journal since, as a practical matter, it's contained within the
longer URL for the hypertext published under its auspices. However, if any special circumstances are involved, if, for example,
the journal's web address has changed and the article you are citing is stored at its old address, you should explain that in a discursive footnote.

Discursive footnotes will be needed in the CMS, the MLA, and
the APA in-text citation and work-cited methods. The parenthetical references to the source should, where the page number would
go in a print citation, give the filename, which ends the URL that
leads to the web page you are citing. For example, note the parenthetical reference at the end of this quote: "If we are not to abro-
gate our role as teachers completely, we need to find flexible tools
that can involve students in the incompletely-understood environment that is (or maybe isn't) growing up around them" (Brent
1997, TEACHGEN.HTM).[1] The discursive note might read:

[1]All citations from Doug Brent's hypertext, "Rhetorics of the Web: Implications for Teachers of Literacy," will include, in place of page numbers, the name of the file being quoted from or referred to. Brent's piece is a hypertext made up of 61 files with no page numbers. The first page a reader accesses to begin the hypertext is (http://english.ttu.edu/kairos/2.1/features/brent/wayin.htm). To go directly to the filed cited, place the filename in the last part of the URL. Thus to get to TEACHGEN.HTM, you would enter the following in your browser: (http://english.ttu.edu/kairos/2.1/features/ brent/TEACHGEN.HTM). Filenames are given exactly as they appear.

The explanatory footnote should be used the first time you refer to a hypertext. For each new hypertext cited, provide a discursive footnote that explains the hypertext and its URL structure. With a little care and a little explaining, you can reliably cite a hypertext. We've also found that using the filenames in the parenthetical reference is useful while drafting, making it easier to return to a page to double-check your notes or rethink your own arguments. If you put your essay on the Web, instead of an explanatory footnote, link directly to the page cited in the hypertext.

To get a sense of how rich and interconnected a hypertext can be, in structure and form, you should take a look at *Kairos* and other sites on the Web that create complex hypertexts. For fiction examples, try *Hyperizons: the Hypertext Fiction Homepage* (http://www.duke.edu/~mshumate/hyperfic.html).

16

Learning Online: A List of Resources

CHAPTER CONTENTS

The Internet sites listed in this section represent only a sampling of the resources available for English majors to use. Since the study of English literature and writing can take you to a variety of subjects, this list of resources will do the same. We begin with resources for conducting searches, then move to subject-categorized databases, and from there into particular areas relevant to English majors. For gopher-based resources, we provide the gopher information as well as its World Wide Web URL. In Chapter 17, we list resources for learning more about the Internet, the World Wide Web, and for getting Internet tools.

16.1 Searches

Direct (or keyword) searches

FTP Gateways and Archie Searches
gopher://gopher.tc.umn.edu:70/11/FTP%20Searches

Veronica Search
This search helps you find Gopher directory titles. Useful search words might include "Shakespeare," "Literature," or "Computers and Writing."
gopher://gopher.tc.umn.edu:70/11/
Other%20Gopher%20and%20Information%20Servers/

WAIS-Based Information
gopher://gopher-gw.micro.umn.edu:70/11/WAISes

All In One Search http://www.albany.net/~wcross/
all1srch.html
Allows you to search many sites — WWW, FTP servers, gopher — by subject.

Digital's Search Program http://www.altavista.digital.com/

Lycos Search http://www.lycos.com

Metacrawler Search
http://metacrawler.cs.washington.edu:8080/index.html

WebCrawler Search http://webcrawler.com/

WWW Worm Search
http://www.cs.colorado.edu/home/mcbryan/WWWW.html

Undirected searches

URouLette http://www.uroulette.com:8000/
Spin the wheel and go to random Web sites.

Subject-categorized search resources

Subject-categorized searches take you to sites with topic or subject headings. Many of these work on a tree-branch model, starting with broad categories or topics and then narrowing the categories down in more detailed links or subdirectories. These areas are fun to browse. Remember to use your bookmarking feature if you find something you like and plan to return to.

Gopher Jewels
gopher://cwis.usc.edu:70/11/

Other_Gophers_and_Information_Resources/
Gophers_by_Subject/Gopher_Jewels

PEG, a Peripatetic, Eclectic GOPHER
This is a neat place to browse; it is maintained by Calvin
Boyer of the University of California-Irvine Office of Academic Computing.
gopher://peg.cwis.uci.edu:7000/11/gopher.welcome/peg/

Awesome Lists http://www.clark.net/pub/journalism/
awesome.html
These are lists John Makulovich developed for journalists and
for training people on how to use the Internet. These are useful for English majors because many journalism courses fall
under English departments, and journalism, like English literature, and writing, covers many fields.

**The University of Michigan's Subject-Categorized Internet
Resources**
http://www.lib.umich.edu/chhome.html

The World Wide Web Virtual Library
http://www.w3.org/hypertext/DataSources/bySubject/
Overview.html

The Yahoo Directory http://www.yahoo.com/

Webliography http://www.lib.lsu.edu/weblio.html
Steven R. Harris is a librarian at Louisiana State University.
His collection of resources is intended to be of aid to aca-
demic searching.

16.2   English Departments and Courses

This category of resources includes information on other online
English departments. You can do anything from investigating
graduate school programs to seeing what other students are doing on the Internet with classwork.

English and Humanities Departments Online
http://www.academic.marist.edu/otherdep.htm
There are a lot of collections online of English departments
and their resources and programs, but the best one we have
found so far is maintained by Tom Goldpaugh, an Assistant
Professor of English at Marist College.

The Literary Research Guide's List of Online Courses
http://www.english.upenn.edu/~jlynch/syllabi.html

Syllabi for literature courses using the Internet.

Writing for the World
http://icarus.uic.edu/~kdorwick/world.html

Writing Classes on the Web
http://ernie.bgsu.edu/~skrause/WWW__Classes/

World Lecture Hall
http://www.utexas.edu/world/lecture/

Voice of the Shuttle
http://humanitas.ucsb.edu/shuttle/eng-c.html
Syllabi and teaching resources for English literature and writing courses.

16.3   Scholarly Societies

The Alliance for Computer and Writing (ACW) Homepage
http://english.ttu.edu/acw/
An excellent source for seeing what writing teachers and students are doing on the Internet; includes helpful links for beginners. As a professional organization, it also offers support to teachers, including advice, sample syllabi, software reviews, bibliographies, and conference information.

Association of Teachers of Technical Writing
http://english.ttu.edu/ATTW/

List of Home Pages of Scholarly Societies and Associations
http://www.lib.uwaterloo.ca/society/overview.html

Modern Humanities Research Association (MHRA)
http://www.hull.ac.uk/Hull/FR__Web/mhra.html
Of special use is the MHRA's ABELL: The Annual Bibliography of English Language and Literature
(http://www.hull.ac.uk/Hull/FR__Web/abell.html).

National Council of Teachers of English (NCTE)
http://www.note.org/

Scholarly Information Resources
http://www.lib.lsu.edu/general/scholar.html

Writing Across the Curriculum (WAC) Homepage
http://ewu66649.ewu.edu/WAC.html

The Internet Public Library
This is a great resource that treats the Internet like a library
and organizes information along library terms. The sites
listed in this resource have been carefully chosen. A good
place to start your research or look for quality sources.
http://www.ipl.org/

The Library of Congress's Library Gateway
A list of libraries with online catalogues accessible via the
WWW.
http://lcweb.loc.gov/z3950/gateway.htm

16.4   E-Mail Directories

The Kovacs Directory

The best place to learn about lists for discussion is from *The Directory of Scholarly Electronic Conferences,* edited by Diane Kovacs
and The Directory Team. Electronic conferences include e-mail
discussion lists, online journals and newsletters, Usenet groups,
MOOs, and other real-time conferencing programs used by
scholars. To access the Kovacs Directory, via the WWW, you can
use the following address:

http://www.n2h2.com/KOVACS/

Other recommended directories

Liszt Directory of E-Mail Discussion Groups
http://www.liszt.com

Tile.Net/Listserv Reference to Internet Discussion Groups
http://tile.net/tile/listserv/

16.5   Usenet Groups for Writing and Literature

These discussion groups about writing, words, teaching writing,
and literature do not represent an exhaustive list, but they are a
good place to start. If your school does not access one of these
lists, contact your system administrator and ask him or her to include it in the Usenet listings for the campus.

General writing

misc.writing
Miscellaneous writing is a deceiving name. We tend to think of "miscellaneous," as we do "etcetera" and "whatever," as an afterthought. Think of this group as a miscellany, a compendium of topics, insights, and contentions about writing from a variety of writers.

Specialized writing

misc.writing.screenplays
Discusses both the writing and selling of screenplays.

alt.stagecraft
This group discusses technical aspects of theater production. If you're writing plays, this will be a useful resource for insight into how your work might be produced.

bit.listserv.techwr-l
Technical writing discussion list. This group has technical writers and technical writing instructors and students on it. It's a good mix of people from the professions and the schools.

alt.graffiti
Yes, a discussion of graffiti. To what extent are some pages on the WWW a kind of virtual graffiti?

The English language

alt.usage.english
This group covers all kinds of peculiarities in English. It's entertaining because the issues almost always include some difference in interpretation of rules of usage, a sign of the vitality of the English language.

bit.listserv.words-1
A discussion of word histories, origins, and uses in English, both spoken and written.

alt.humor.puns
You might roll your eyes and wince while downloading some of these gems, but if you like wordplay, you'll want to visit this newsgroup.

Literature and authors

bit.listserv.literary
Literary covers a wide range of topics having to do with the interpretation and enjoyment of literature. If you think of interpretation and enjoyment as separate, this list shows they are not.

Writing in computer-dependent forums

comp.infosystems.www.authoring.html
Writing HTML for the World Wide Web. The questions and advice range from novice to expert. This is a good place to start learning about HTML.

alt.hypertext
For discussing issues in hypertext writing; conversation covers practice and theory.

16.6   Literature and the Humanities

The American Studies Web
http://www.cis.yale.edu/~davidp/amstud.html
This is the best place to start if you're looking for Internet sources on American studies, including literature, history, culture, and politics.

A Directory of Medieval Studies Resources
http://www.georgetown.edu/labyrinth/Virtual__Library/Medieval__Studies.html
This links to archives of manuscripts, discussion lists, and articles on Medieval literature and history.

A Directory of Humanities Resources on the Internet
http://www.lib.lsu.edu/weblio.htm1#Humanities
This is one of the subcategories in Stephen Harris's Web-liography.

The Carnegie Mellon English Server
http://english-server.hss.cmu.edu/
This resource is excellent and extensive.

Literary Research Tools on the Net
http://www.english.upenn.edu/~jlynch/lit
This is one of the most thorough and useful resources on the Internet.

Literature in Electronic Format
http://www.jsu.edu/depart/english/choice.htm
This site takes you to resources discussed in "Literature
in Electronic Format," an essay by Joanne E. Gates
published in the April 1997 issue of *Choice*. This is a wonderful bibliographic essay that surveys CD-ROM and Internet-based repositories of American and British literature,
176 resources in all. We recommend you get a copy of the
essay.

An Introduction to the Study of Literature
http://www.uwm.edu/People/jat/
Written and maintained by Jane Thompson, this site offers
high school and college students "definitions of literary
terms, brief explanations of a variety of literary theories,
directions for doing various kinds of literary analysis, and
links to other resources on the Web."

16.7 Writing

Internet Writers Resource Guide from Bricolage
http://bel.avonibp.co.uk/bricolage/resources/lounge/IWRG/
index.html
An extensive guide with links to professional writer's
groups, information on contracts and copyright, and genre-
specific advice (children's fiction, science fiction, short
story).

Writer's Resources on the Web
http://www.interlog.com/~ohi/www/writesource.html
Part of the World Wide Web Virtual Library, this page catego-
rizes information for writers and on writing by subject. A very
thorough resource.

The Word
http://www.speakeasy.org/~dbrick/Hot/word.html
An eclectic collection of links that cover writing resources,
magazines, journals, and reference works.

The National Writing Centers Association (NWCA)
http://www2.colgate.edu/diw/NWCA.html

The NWCA's List of Online Writing Labs and Centers
http://www2.colgate.edu/diw/NWCAOWLS.html

16.8 MOO and MUD Resources

Diversity University MOO telnet moo.du.org 8888
Teachers can bring classes here.

CollegeTown MOO telnet patty.bvu.edu 7777
An online, college model MOO.

Connections MOO telnet oz.net 3333
A MOO for teachers and students to come as a class or on
their own; friendly, supportive, and fun.

Virtual Online University telnet brazos.iac.net 8888
A liberal arts university offering courses for credit; it is a
model for distance education.

VOUMOO Web Page http://www.athena.edu/index.html

University of Missouri's ZooMOO
telnet showme.missouri.edu 8888
Lots of projects by English classes.

ZooMoo Web Page http://www.missouri.edu:80/~moo/

Help for MOOs and MUDS

CMC Forums by John December
http://www.rpi.edu/Internet/Guides/decemj/itools/cmc.html
Covers MOOs, MUDs, and a whole lot more.

The MOO Central Help Page by Jeffrey R. Galin
http://www.pitt.edu/~jrgst7/MOOcentral.html
Excellent source for educational uses of MOOs, with telnet
links to a wide variety of MOOs.

Lydia Leong's Information on MUDs/MOOs/MUSHs
http://www.cis.upenn.edu/~lwl/mudinfo.html
One of the most authoritative sites; good links to research on
MUDs, MOOs, and MUSHs (multiuser simulated hallucina-
tions).

Frequently Asked Questions: MUD Clients and Servers
http://www.cs.okstate.edu/~jds/mudfaq-p2.html
Written by Jennifer Smith, this is the best place to learn about
MUD and MOO clients. The links will take you directly to the
clients described.

16.9 Publications

Publication directories

A Directory of Scholarly Publications
http://www.georgetown.edu/labyrinth/professional/pubs/
scholarly__pubs.html
Educational Resources Information Center (ERIC)
ERIC is one of the leading databases and resources for education and education-related articles.
http://www.aspensys.com/eric/index.html
gopher://ericir.syr.edu:70/11/Clearinghouses/16houses/CLL

The Gutenberg E-Text Homepage
http://jg.cso.uiuc.edu/PG/Welcome.html
The following links are from Carnegie Mellon's English Server:

A Directory of Online Journals and Periodicals
http://english.hss.cmu.edu/Journals.html

A Directory of Online Books by Author
http://www.cs.cmu.edu:8001/Web/bookauthors.html

A Directory of Online Books
http://www.cs.cmu.edu/Web/books.htm

Banned Books Online
http://www.cs.cmu.edu/Web/People/spok/banned-
books.html
A great (and sobering) resource on censorship.

Online Reference Works
http://www.cs.cmu.edu:8001/Web/references.html

Directories to online journals and magazines

Alex: A Catalogue of Electronic Texts on the Internet
http://www.lib.ncsu.edu:80/stacks/alex-index.html

CIC Electronic Journals Collection
http://ejournals.cic.net

Ejournal SiteGuide: a MetaSource
http://unixg.ubc.ca:7001/0/providers/hss/zjj/ejhome.html

Electronic Magazines
http://www.abc.hu/unix/magazines.html

The Electronic Newsstand
http://enews.com/

Scholarly Journals Distributed Via the World Wide Web
http://info.lib.uh.edu/wj/webjour.html

WWW Virtual Library Electronic Journals Catalog
http://www.edoc.com/ejournal

Yahoo List of Lists of Electronic Magazines
http://www.yahoo.com/Entertainment/Magazines/Indices

Online journals: a sampling

Kairos: A Journal for Teachers of Writing in Webbed Environments
http://english.ttu.edu/kairos/
A new online journal for teachers and advanced students who are using the World Wide Web in writing classes.

RhetNet, a Cyberjournal for Rhetoric and Writing
http://www.missouri.edu/~rhetnet
An exploratory publication that intentionally takes the shape of the Net rather than replicating print conventions of form and content. Its contents include threads of conversation culled from mailing list discussions.

Computer-Mediated Communication Magazine
http://www.december.com/cmc/mag/current/toc.html

Post-Modern Culture, An Electronic Journal of Interdisciplinary Criticism
http://jefferson.village.virginia.edu/pmc/contents.all.html

The Trincoll Journal
http://www.trincoll.edu/tj/trincolljournal.html
This is written and produced by students at Trinity College in Hartford, Connecticut.

Online magazines: a sampling

The Atlantic Monthly
http://www2.theatlantic.com/Atlantic/

HotWired
http://www.hotwired.com/
The online companion to *Wired*, a magazine that focuses on technology and culture.

Internet World
http://pubs.iworld.com/iw-online/index.html

Mother Jones
http://www.mojones.com/
A progressive, investigative journal.

Nando.Net, a News Service from McClatchy New Media
http://www2.nando.net/

The New York Times
http://www.nytimes.com/

The New York Times Book Review
http://www.nytimes.com/books/

Time Warner's Pathfinder Web News Service
http://pathfinder.com/
Links to *Time, Entertainment Weekly, People* and other magazines.

The Utne Lens
http://www.utne.com/

Who Cares Magazine
http://www.whocares.org/themag.html
An online journal of community service ideas and issues.

16.10 Government Resources

The Library of Congress
http://lcweb.loc.gov/
The library is in the process of digitizing some of its best
collections. For example, you can access the Federal Writer's
Folklore Project interviews conducted from 1936 to 1940.

Thomas: Legislative Information
http://thomas.loc.gov/
Includes information on pending bills, committee assignments, and homepages of representatives.

The U.S. Department of Education
http://www.ed.gov/
Great resources for learning about grants, Goals 2000, inno-
vative educational practices, and links to other education resources.

The White House
http://www.whitehouse.gov/
Connect to the White House and find position statements
and press releases among the information.

17

Help with the Internet

This list contains resources for learning more about the Internet and the World Wide Web.

17.1 Online Books About the Internet

Daniel J. Barrett, *Bandits on the Information Superhighway.* O'Reilly and Associates.
http://www.ora.com/gnn/bus/ora/item/bandits.html

John December. *Internet Web Text — A Guide to the Internet.*
http://www.rpi.edu/Internet/Guides/decemj/text.html

Mark Harrison. *The USENET Handbook.* O'Reilly and Associates.
http://www.ora.com/gnn/bus/ora/item/useneth.html

Tanya Herlick and Michael Bauer. *Internet Basics.*
http://www.sen.ca.gov/www/leginfo/docs/orient/
help1__intro.html

Ed Krol, adapted by Bruce Klopfenstein. *The Whole Internet User's Guide & Catalog, Academic Edition.*
http://www.ora.com/gnn/bus/ora/item/twi2aca.html

Linda Lamb and Jerry Peek. *Using E-mail Effectively.* O'Reilly and Associates.
http://www.ora.com/gnn/bus/ora/item/usemail.html

David W. Sanderson. *Smileys.* O'Reilly and Associates.
http://www.ora.com/gnn/bus/ora/item/smileys.html

Victor Vitanza. *CyberReader*. Allyn and Bacon, 1996.
http://www.abacon.com/cyber/public_html/cyber.html

17.2   Printed Books About the Internet

Bill Junor and Chris DeMontravel. *Internet: The User's Guide for Everyone*. Branden Books, 1995.

Dave Taylor. *Creating Cool Web Pages with HTML*. IDG Books, 1995.

Victor Vitanza. *CyberReader*. Allyn and Bacon, 1996.

17.3   Other Online Internet Guides

Newbie Net Internation Home Page
http://www.Newbie.NET/
"Helping anybody learn the basic skills needed to tap into the tremendous wealth of information residing in that big virtual thingie called the Internet is the core of our mission." The site features a cybercourse as well as directions on how to join an e-mail list where you can ask any, and they do mean *any*, question about using the Internet.

Computers: Internet Beginner's Guides
http://www.yahoo.com/Computers/Internet/Beginner_s_Guide/
From the Yahoo directory.

17.4   Help with the World Wide Web

HTML Tutorial — Overview
http://www-pcd.stanford.edu/mogens/intro/tutorial.html
We recommend starting here for step-by-step directions. This resource is maintained by Christian Mogensen of Stanford University.

WWW for Newbies
http://www.pitt.edu/~jrgst7/newbie.html
By Jeffrey R. Galin, whose pages are among the most user friendly.

Resources for Learning About SGML & HTML
http://www.lib.lsu.edu/hum/sgml.html
Compiled by Steven R. Harris.

Maricopa Center for Learning and Instruction
http://www.mcli.dist.maricopa.edu/
A site with instructional material for those who are relatively new to the Internet, including how-to files on creating web documents. One of the best resources for teachers and students on the World Wide Web.

Computers: World Wide Web Beginner's Guide
http://www.yahoo.com/Computers/World_Wide_Web/
Beginner_s_Guides/
From the Yahoo directory.

World Wide Web Consortium Homepage
http://WWW.w3.org/
Sources about writing and working in the WWW, as well as links to useful sites.

A Timeline Tracing the Development of the Web
http://WWW.w3.org/hypertext/WWW/History.html
You'll be amazed at how far and how quickly the WWW has developed.

Computers and Writing Research at Lab — The University of Texas
http://www.en.utexas.edu/
This is an eclectic array of resources, including tutorials and helps sheets, links to scholarly articles about teaching in computer environments, and links to student web pages. A good place to go to see what other students are doing.

The World Wide Web Unleashed
http://www.rpi.edu/~decemj/works/wwwu.html
An online hypertext book by John December and Neil Randall. One of the most thorough WWW resources you'll ever find. Check out the Index when you get there.

17.5 Sites for Internet Tools

Web browsers

Netscape Communications' Homepage
http://home.Netscape.com/

NCSA Mosaic's Homepage
http://www.ncsa.uiuc.edu/SDG/Software/Mosaic/
NCSAMosaicHome.html

Microsoft's Internet Explorer
http://www.microsoft.com

Other Internet tools

GIFConverter Site
http://www.kamit.com/gifconverter.html
A software tool for viewing and converting graphics. Useful for web designing or for those with nongraphic browsers who choose to download images to their own computer.

Java Site
http://www.javasoft.com/index.html
Java is a programming language for advanced users. It's in this introductory guide because if you're truly interested in learning more about the Internet for your own personal or academic use, you'll want to know about Java.

Merit Software Archives
gopher://gopher.archive.merit.edu:70/11/.software-archives
Here you will find software for both Macintosh and PC formats.

Washington University Archives
http://wuarchive.wustl.edu/
A huge collection of documents and software.

18

An Overview of Writing Collaborative Hypertexts

18.1 Introduction

Collaborative hypertext is the ability to connect, via a URL, to other material on the Web, with a click of the mouse. By agreeing to a hypertext transfer protocol (HTTP) and a hypertext markup language (HTML), web writers can link information and create myriad paths for readers to follow. Collaborative hypertext is what makes the Web possible.

Most writing on the Web, however, consists primarily of print-based, linear essays with occasional links. Very little on the Web is what Stuart Moulthrop, a noted hypertext author and theorist, calls native hypertext. Instead of writing an essay and then adding a few links as an afterthought, the hypertext writer conceives an essay with lots of links and pages already in mind. Instead of working from an outline, with its ordered, by-the-numbers progression, a hypertext writer seeks a matrix of connections, with paths and overlaps that resemble a spider's web.

Although it is quite possible to construct such a web on your own, we recommend collaboratively writing web-based hypertexts. A good, content-rich site, with lots of links and good topic coverage, can be created sooner and more thoroughly working with a team than it can toiling alone. In this chapter, we provide a brief overview of this kind of extensive and more ambitious project.

18.2   Why Collaborate?

Since we concede that initially collaboration takes more effort than working alone, especially when creating a collaborative hypertext, you may be wondering why it's worth doing. Here are some answers.

We learn from others

People naturally learn from being around other people, whether a family, a neighborhood, a classroom, or a church. When group members work well together their shared perspectives and ideas create deeper and wider understanding. This is the very principle that drives academic inquiry. Collaborative writing takes what we do naturally and emphasizes it.

Co-authoring is a valued skill

Andrea Lunsford and Lisa Ede's remarkable study of workplace writing, *Singular Texts/Plural Authors: Perspectives on Collaborative Writing* (Carbondale: Southern Illinois Press, 1990) explores the complexities and importance collaborative writing has in many workplaces. Collaborative writing in print-based forms is already important in today's workplace. There is every reason to believe that it will become even more important for electronic-based writing.

Collaboration can enhance individuality

To work well in a group, you must articulate clearly and tactfully what you think. You need to listen carefully and generously to what your co-authors think. To do all these well, you need to have a good sense of yourself; you need confidence, patience, and humor. Working collaboratively can help you develop these skills and traits. There's no guarantee that such will happen, but the chance to collaborate makes it possible in ways that writing alone cannot.

Intellectual collaboration fosters intellectual community

For intellectual communities to thrive, members must share their intellectual insights. We have very detailed legal and ethical systems for citing sources, acknowledging intellectual debts, and purchasing copyrights that are meant to make this sharing fair and workable across the global village the Internet spans. However, those details can sometimes get in the way of the spirit of intellectual sharing. It's hard to feel a part of an intellectual community when your only access to it is by a very prescriptive set of rules. We thus encourage you to collaborate side-by-side, sleeves rolled-up, so that you can participate in an intellectual community on a small village scale by building a shared intellectual project — the web site you create with your fellow writers.

Working with others is fun

We always save our favorite reason for last. Our favorite reason for doing collaborative work is that it's usually fun and rewarding. It's rarely easy, but with a good group of people who are open to one another's ideas and willing to take responsibility for their share of the work, it can be exhilarating. It's also a great way to cement friendships.

18.3   Organizing a Collaborative Hypertext

Get to know your co-authors

An e-mail distribution list makes this possible across distance and time — that way you can keep in touch outside class. In the first few weeks of e-mail and face-to-face meetings, the best thing is to generate lots of possibilities; don't reject any ideas too soon. Think of these first few meetings and e-mailing rounds as group brainstorming or interactive freewriting. For example, if your group is going to write about adjusting to college, your first round of e-mail might be to exchange stories about the first week of school. The stories both contribute to the project and help you get to know one another.

Find an audience and a purpose

Your project will be published on the Web where audiences can find it. Choose an audience *you know* and whose needs you can anticipate. This will help you determine the balance between what needs to be said and how it needs to be presented. If your group decides to write a hypertext about adjusting to the first year of college, would your audience be high school seniors?

Would it be parents of freshmen? What would your purpose be? Would it be to help high school seniors plan? Would it be survival tips for distraught parents? Would it be all the above?

Let your audience and purpose guide your planning

Once you have an audience and purpose, you'll more easily begin to generate useful questions and ideas for planning. Let's suppose your audience is high school seniors who will be going to your college, and your purpose is to make the transition as easy and successful as possible. Someone might want to emphasize academics, someone else might want to cover dorm life, someone else might want to cover the off-campus scene, and someone else might want to cover support services. There are many more possibilities, but you have only so much time and so much you can cover well.

For our sample project, the "Adjusting to the First Year" web site, there will be disagreements about what's best. Collaborative hypertext allows you to create projects where one uniform view is not required. To work together, you do not have to agree at all times on all things. Multiple perspectives give a fuller picture of the complexity of an issue. A collaborative hypertext can include — and be enhanced by — diverse views.

Assign tasks and duties: set up a schedule

Generate a list of what needs to be done. Possibilities for our sample project include researching the first-year experience (interviews with classmates, looking at school policies, analyzing the campus tour and promotional literature); planning the management of the hypertext itself (how will the files be written, stored, and peer reviewed?); and assigning hypertext production roles (proofreader, a person to make sure all the links work, graphics checker). Assign a manager to keep track of what needs to be done and who will be doing it. It is important to be both flexible and firm. The group needs the flexibility to reassign tasks or rethink a plan, but it also needs to be firm about meeting deadlines. Every member should have a copy of the assignments and deadlines of others. Everyone should anticipate filling multiple roles.

Think in hypertext

The first article to discuss hypertext, Vannevar Bush's 1945 *Atlantic Monthly* essay, "As We May Think" (http://www.theatlantic.

com/atlantic/atlweb/flashbks/computer/Bushf.htm), longed for a hypertext system that made connections in the same way our minds work. Most of us make some of our intellectual connections by association and interlinked thinking. In traditional essays, however, the form — pages with paragraphs that go in a set order — urges us to present thinking in a linear and hierarchical way. Hypertext lets us express ideas in ways that are closer to how we may think.

Many of you may have seen clustering. In clustering, the idea is to think associatively, to expand ideas and branch out. It's a technique many writers use to generate ideas and suggest relationships among the ideas. Figure 18.1 shows a cluster on quiet places to go on campus for our sample web site on adjusting to the first year of college.

The procedure in print would be to turn this map into an essay with a beginning, middle, and end, a noble pursuit to be sure. The procedure in hypertext is not to lose the map, but to enhance it and make it a writing and reading principle. To map

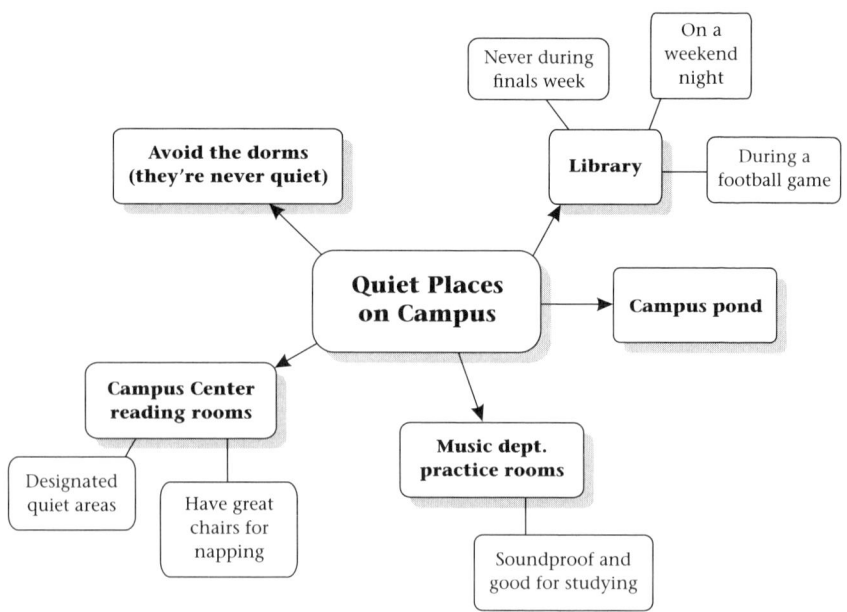

Figure 18.1

hypertext then, we suggest you use the clustering technique in your drafting. Each member of the group should write a hypertext (or two) on his or her area of coverage, with an eye toward linking these smaller hypertexts into a larger whole.

Merge your hypertexts into a larger web site

In this collaborative hypertext model, writers create their own map, their own hypertext cluster, but with the goal of interlinking the clusters and maps into a larger whole. One of the best ways to coordinate this is to distribute copies of the clusters among co-authors. Each author should also distribute the questions he or she is asking about an area of adjusting to the first year of college. Research questions, rhetorical questions, content questions, and goals and thesis statements should be shared early on.

Sharing ideas and drafts at all stages makes your classmates your eyes and ears. They might find something useful for you while they conduct their research. It also lets you know where coverage will overlap. Where overlapping coverage occurs, writers can meet and co-author a single page. Keeping up with each member's progress also lets everyone know where cross links would be good. For example, if one person is writing on dorm rooms and another on food on campus, the food writer might want to link to the dorm writer's page on refrigerators and hot plates. The dorm writer might want to link the food writer's page on "Dorm Favorites: Recipes for Chips, Candy Bars, and Other Vending Machine Delicacies."

Include reader input

There are a number of ways you can do this. You can have e-mail links built into each page; you can use a web-based discussion tool such as Hypernews; or you might even host an e-mail discussion list or campuswide Usenet group. You can add pages that include comments or tips from these lists (with the author's permission, of course). The goal is to make your site interactive so that the collaboration started by your group extends to your readers.

GLOSSARY

* The asterisk is used as a wildcard with commands to mean "all." For example, if in UNIX you wanted to remove a bunch of files that began with th, such as this.01, this.02, and this.03, you could enter **rm th*.0*** and all the files that begin with th would be removed. The asterisk frequently appears as shorthand as well. To refer to MOOs, MUDs, and MUSHs efficiently, people often write M*s.

Alias Sometimes people use this as a synonym for your login name. In that sense, it is short for the phrase ALso Identified AS. However, alias is also a UNIX command. You can create an alias for something you do often. For example, typing **alias daedalus telnet MOO.daedalus.com** 7777 at your prompt creates an alias called daedalus, which performs the same function as typing **telnet MOO.daedalus.com** 7777.

Archie Named after that famed Smallville teen, Archie allows users to search anonymous file transfer protocol (FTP) sites for files.

ARPANet Advanced Research Projects Administration Network. The system that laid the groundwork for the Internet. It was developed by the Department of Defense as a way to allow scientists working on defense projects to transfer data more rapidly. It was also intended as a network that could survive a nuclear war, a feat accomplished by assuring there was no central, controlling computer.

Article A synonym for an e-mail message posted to Usenet, sometimes referred to simply as a post.

ASCII American Standard Code for Information Interchange. This code is used for writing numbers, letters, and symbols without formatting particular to one word processing or editing program. A useful equivalent found on most word processors is the option to save a file as text only.

Bandwidth   The amount of data a line can move. As we move to fiber optics, we increase bandwidth — more data can be moved at faster speeds.

BBS   Bulletin Board System. An electronic meeting place organized by software that allows users to exchange mail, hold discussions, and swap files. Some BBSs offer Internet access, such as America Online, Prodigy, and CompuServe.

Binhex   BINary HEXadecimal. It converts nontext files into ASCII. This allows these files, often software, to be e-mailed. Binhex is a format associated with Macintosh, and many files found in Mac software archives are in binhex format with an .hqx file extension as part of their name. To use these files, they have to be "unbinhexed" — converted from ASCII to nontext format — after you download them to your Mac.

Bit   Binary digIT. The smallest part of computer data. Binary systems rely on a combination of 1s and 0s to create a bit. Bits combine to form bytes. Bits are also used as a way to measure bandwidth (how much information can be moved); a modem, for example, may operate at 9,600 bps, or bits per second.

BITNET   Because It's Time NETwork. BITNET is one of the original academic networks, but now much of BITNET has switched to the Internet's .edu domain. BITNET is still in place, and e-mail can move freely between BITNET and Internet.

Browser   A program that allows you to "see" and use Internet tools. For example, Mosaic is a World Wide Web browser that lets you navigate and see what's on the World Wide Web (see also *client*).

Byte   About 8 to 10 bits make a byte. Bytes combine to make other data, such as words.

CDA (Communications Decency Act)   An effort by the U.S. government to protect children from pornographic material found on the Internet. The appropriateness of the law was vigorously debated on the Net and in the popular media. Some argued that it was the best way to protect children from indecent material. Others asserted that it violated adults' constitutional rights to free speech and that other means of protecting children would be as effective. The courts eventually ruled that the law was too restrictive, and it was overturned.

Client   Software that reaches into the Internet and can bring things back for you. Gopher is a good example. In gopher, links to other sights are already made for you and presented in a numbered menu. Gopher also contains components that allow you to download or mail what you find. Sometimes a client will bring you to files, and sometimes it will bring you to other software — ERIC, for example, or a BBS — which you must then log on to.

CMC   Computer Mediated Communication. This refers to tools used via a computer to communicate with others. CMC is generally broken into two broad categories, synchronous (realtime) and asynchronous. E-mail, BBS postings, Usenet, file sharing are examples of asynchronous. That means the communication happens over time. A message posted to a discussion list is not likely to be read by everyone on the list the second you post it.

Real-time or synchronous CMC includes CUSEEME (realtime videoconferencing) software, MOOs, MUDs, IRC, and in some classrooms, products such as Daedalus's Interchange, Norton's Connect, or Houghton Mifflin's CommonSpace.

Cyberspace   Coined by William Gibson in his novel *Neuromancer,* most people use the word to describe the Internet or other virtual environments (such as BBSs, LANs, and MOOs). The metaphor implies limitless, formless, and ultimately unknowable space that invites us to explore it. Compare that to a metaphor like the information superhighway, and you can begin to see how metaphors really go a long way in determining how we think about and, ultimately, use computers.

Domain Name System   Sometimes referred to as DNS, it is a method for identifying an Internet host computer. The domain name uses words and abbreviations to correspond to router numbers assigned to the domain. The ending tells you about the type of site the domain is. Common endings are:

edu	for educational
gov	for government
com	for a business or person accessing from a commercial provider
ca	for Canada
Net	often for an Internet service provider
uk	for United Kingdom
org	usually for a nonprofit organization

Elm   Electronic mail for UNIX. Elm is freeware, which means you can get a copy and use it at no cost.

Ethernet   A networking method that allows computers to share data. Ethernet is used to describe a range of network wiring methods and speeds. In essence, Ethernet is like the switching station at a busy railroad terminal. It determines the speed and order of data movement.

FAQs   Frequently Asked Questions. FAQs list and answer the most common questions on a particular subject. Usually the subject is a Usenet group or discussion list, but it can also be about software or an Internet site.

Flame   In computer mediated communication (CMC) — e-mail and chat programs — a flame, at its worst and most obvious, is an invective, acrimonious, ad hominen, intolerant, and scurrilous message. However, many times, mild disagreements are taken as flames when no flaming was intended. Often flames occur because a message meant as ironic or sarcastic is mistaken for intentional.

FTP   File Transfer Protocol. A protocol, or method, for transferring a file from one computer to another via the Internet. FTP allows a user to log on to another Internet site for retrieving a file there. Many Internet sites provide publicly accessible archives that anyone can access by using the login name "anonymous."

Gopher   A menued system for accessing information on the Internet. Usually accessed by typing **gopher** at your account prompt, the software allows universities and other sites to link to other information and also to organize their own information for visitors and people on their campus.

Host   A computer that is directly connected to the Internet. For most of you, it is the computer at your school on which you have your account. When you use your account, you are accessing the host and are allowed to run certain programs and services that are stored on the host, such as gopher or an e-mail program.

HTML   HyperText Markup Language. The coding language that creates hypertext documents for use on the World Wide Web. HTML works by inserting directions in and around text for web browsers to follow when they access a page.

HTTP   HyperText Transport Protocol. The protocol for linking to files in hypertext format. HTTP is the main protocol used in the World Wide Web (WWW).

Hypertext   A system for organizing information in nodes and links. In hypertext, a node is a segment of information; on the World Wide Web, nodes are called pages. Within a page, a writer can create a link. The link can lead to another page; another Internet service or site such as gopher or FTP; or a graphic image, audio clip, or video clip.

Internet The "too vast to accurately count" connection of computers and computer networks around the world. When you are on the Internet, you are on the network that evolved from the ARPANet project and are accessing via a machine that follows TCP/IP protocols.

internet Short for internetwork. Any two or more networks that are connected are internetworked, and thus form an internet. Some internets are connected to the Internet. There are many internets, but only one Internet.

IP Internet Protocol. The rules that determine how information travels on the Internet and how the collection of computers is networked. Often found in other acronyms such as SLIP or TCP/IP.

IP Number A particular number assigned to an Internet host. No two hosts share the same number. Since numbers are hard to remember, most numbers receive a corresponding domain name. However, more than one domain name can be linked to a number.

IRC Internet Relay Chat. A huge, largely ungoverned Internet-based chat system. It works by accessing IRC servers (and there are a number of them). The servers are linked to one another. Once linked, a user can create a channel or join already created channels. Then, any message a user writes and sends to the channel will be seen almost instantaneously by other users who are on the same channel. Likewise, the user will see any messages other users send. In this way, users can swap messages or chat. The servers relay the messages. IRC is an example of synchronous or real-time computer mediated communication (CMC).

Kilobyte A thousand bytes. Actually it's 1024 bytes, but everyone rounds it off. Often written as just K, as in "I downloaded a 19K file" (see also *byte, bit*).

LAN Local Area Network. A computer network with a short reach, usually the networking of computers in one area such as a building or classroom. If a LAN becomes linked to a larger network, such as the Internet, it is sometimes referred to as a WAN, or wide area network. However, it might help to think in more geographic terms: LAN, one room or building; WAN, one location or company, as on a college campus; and Internet, beyond one room, certainly, but also beyond one institution's domain.

Listproc Software for managing e-mail distribution lists.

Listserv Popular e-mail list distribution software. Listserv originated on BITNET lists, and if you access Usenet, you'll see many groups in the bit.listserv.* hierarchy. This reflects that origin; however, not all those groups (bit.listserv.mbu-1, for example) are BITNET based. In fact, MBU is now Internet based and uses listproc software.

Login   As an adjective, it usually describes some part of the login procedure: "What is your login name?" As a noun, it usually refers to the place in a program or protocol where you do the logging in: "Go to the login and enter your username."

Megabyte   A million bytes. A thousand kilobytes. Often written as just MB, as in "I installed a 2MB software program" (see also *byte, bit, kilobyte*).

Modem   MOdulator, DEModulator. A device that allows your computer to use a phone line so that your computer can access other computers.

MOO   MUD, Object Oriented. The key here is object oriented. A MOO, like a MUD, is primarily a text-based, multiple-user program. Object oriented refers to object-oriented programming, which allows programmers to integrate pieces of programming from other programs into their own designs.

Mosaic   A graphic web browser.

MUD   MultiUser Dungeon, or Dimension. "Dimension" is a more recent, more system-manager-friendly term. "Dungeon" is the original term because the first MUDs were used to play Dungeons and Dragons.

Multimedia   Documents, programs, and products (CD-ROM encyclopedias, for example) that include different kinds of media — text, graphics, audio, and moving images — to convey information. When the information is more integrated and tied to a hypertext system, the term *hypermedia* might be used.

Netscape   The successor to Mosaic as the most popular program for accessing the WWW.

Network   Two or more computers that are connected and can share resources constitute a network.

Newsgroups   The names for discussion groups on Usenet.

NIC   Network Information Center. Any office that manages network information. In colleges, similar duties might be assigned to OIT (Office of Instructional Technologies) or UCS (University Computing Services). That is, not every site uses the term. The most famous, and perhaps most important, NIC is InterNIC, which registers new domain names for computers as they come onto the Internet.

NNTP   Network News Transfer Protocol. Not something you'll ever have to worry about, but you might see it referred to. It's the method used to send Usenet messages.

Node   Any single computer on a network. In some hypertext lexicons, nodes refer to units of information.

Packet   A collection of data. Information is broken into packets, usually about 1500 bytes long, which traverse the Internet independently. Each packet has the address of where it came from and where it's going. Packets share data lines with other packets, much the way commuters share a subway ride. As packets arrive at their destination, they regroup to form the entire set of information.

Password   What you need to know to log on to some systems. A good password is your best protection against someone using your account. Good passwords use a combination of letters and nonletters. They should not be too simple, like Sick1, and should avoid using numbers significant to a user, such as a birth date or license plate number. A random combination of letters, numbers, and symbols (where allowed) works best, such as H7&B3-Q.

PINE   Program for Internet News and E-mail. A very popular program for sending e-mail and reading Usenet news. It was designed for beginners, but can be set for more advanced uses by experienced users. PINE is also sometimes referred to (though not officially) as Pine Is Not Elm to distinguish it from Elm, an earlier and still popular e-mail program.

Port   This has two meanings. One refers to the physical input/output sockets you see on the back of your computer: one might be for a modem, one for a keyboard, one for a printer. Another use of port is to identify a particular Internet application. For example, many MOO addresses contain a port number. You'll usually see it in the instructions: telnet some.MOO.com 7777. In this example, the 7777 represents the port number.

Post   An individual article sent to a Usenet newsgroup. People sometimes carry this term over and use it for messages sent to e-mail discussion lists (also known as posting).

PPP   Point to Point Protocol. Allows a computer to use a regular telephone line and a modem to make a TCP/IP connection and thus be really and truly on the Internet. PPP is gradually replacing SLIP for this purpose. Many people use a PPP connection with a high-speed modem to take full advantage of the World Wide Web.

Push   A newly emerging (and much hyped) Internet tool. Push technology allows people to have information they are interested in automatically "pushed" to their computers, saving them the trouble of doing searches for the latest information. News and stock quotation updates are two early uses of push technology. If the idea catches on, greater variety could abound, and fast.

RTFM   Read the [fine old Anglo-Saxon word] Manual. A common abbreviation in computerdom, usually used by one annoyed by too many questions.

Server   Software that allows a computer to run programs or make information available to other computers. The term refers to the software or the machine on which the server software is stored.

Signature   A file, usually about five to six lines long, appended to the end of e-mail or Usenet messages. The file will contain a sender's name and e-mail address at a minimum, but just as often includes snail mail addresses, quotes, disclaimers, and every once in a while, a copyright claim (also known as sig. or sig. file).

SLIP   Serial Line Internet Protocol. A method for using a telephone line and modem to connect a computer to the Internet directly and use the Internet fully. SLIP is gradually being replaced by PPP.

Smiley   Smilies, or smiley faces, sometimes called emoticons, provide a visual clue to a writer's intent. Common examples include :-) for happy, :-(for sad, and ;-) for just kidding or humor intended.

TCP/IP   Transmission Control Protocol/Internet Protocol. These combined protocols define the Internet. To really be on the Internet, your computer must have TCP/IP software. Don't fret; this is becoming easier to do as modems become faster; the most recent generation of computers usually include this software in the bundling.

Telnet   A method for connecting to a remote computer and using software or accessing information on that computer.

Terminal   A terminal lets you send commands to a computer that is somewhere else. Usually, your keyboard and display screen or monitor will use software that allows it to emulate a terminal (called, naturally enough, terminal emulation software).

Timeout   What will happen when one computer fails to answer another. If, for example, you telnet to another computer, there may be a wait for the connection to go through. However, if the connection is not made in a set amount of time, you will be timed out and will find yourself back at the prompt from which you launched the telnet command.

tn3270   A version of telnet that interacts properly with IBM mainframes.

UNIX   The most common operating system for servers on the Internet, UNIX has TCP/IP built into it and was designed for multiusers. You do not have to use UNIX to use the Internet, but chances are you will run into it in your travels.

URL   Uniform Resource Locator. The method for writing addresses to any resource that can be accessed via the WWW. The beginning of the URL will indicate the resource type: http = hypertext, gopher = gopher, mailto = allows e-mailing, news = connects to Usenet, telnet = allows user to telnet, ftp = connects to FTP server.

Sample URLs:

http://www.umass.edu/english/nickhome.html
mailto:nickc@english.umass.edu
news:new.newusers.questions
gopher://ericir.syr.edu:70/11/Clearinghouses/16houses/CLL

Usenet   A collection of discussion groups that exchange messages. Usenet is worldwide, decentralized, sometimes anarchic, diverse, and accessible on the Internet though it does predate the Internet. Last time we checked, more than 10,000 newsgroups were on Usenet. Your site may not subscribe to them all.

Veronica   Very Easy Rodent Oriented Net-wide Index to Computerized Archives. A tool on gopher for searching gopher menus by word. It will find directories and files that contain the word you search for.

WAIS   Wide Area Information Search Software that allows the indexing (and searching of those indexes) of information. WAIS ranks search results by relevance to request; subsequent searches can be based on prior searches, allowing a searcher to hone his or her queries.

WAN   Wide Area Network. Any network that extends beyond a single building or campus.

WWW   World Wide Web. A hypertext-based system for navigating the Internet and using all its tools: gopher, FTP, http, telnet, tn3270, Usenet, e-mail, WAIS, MUDs and MOOs, and so on. World Wide Web also refers to the various servers that allow text, video, audio, and graphic files to be combined in hypertext.

INDEX

165

E-Mail and Internet Address Book

Name _____   Name _____
Address _____   Address _____
_____   _____

Name _____   Name _____
Address _____   Address _____
_____   _____

Name _____   Name _____
Address _____   Address _____
_____   _____

Name _____   Name _____
Address _____   Address _____
_____   _____

Name _____   Name _____
Address _____   Address _____
_____   _____

Name _____   Name _____
Address _____   Address _____
_____   _____

Name _____   Name _____
Address _____   Address _____
_____   _____

Name _____   Name _____
Address _____   Address _____
_____   _____

Name _____   Name _____
Address _____   Address _____
_____   _____

Name _____   Name _____
Address _____   Address _____
_____   _____